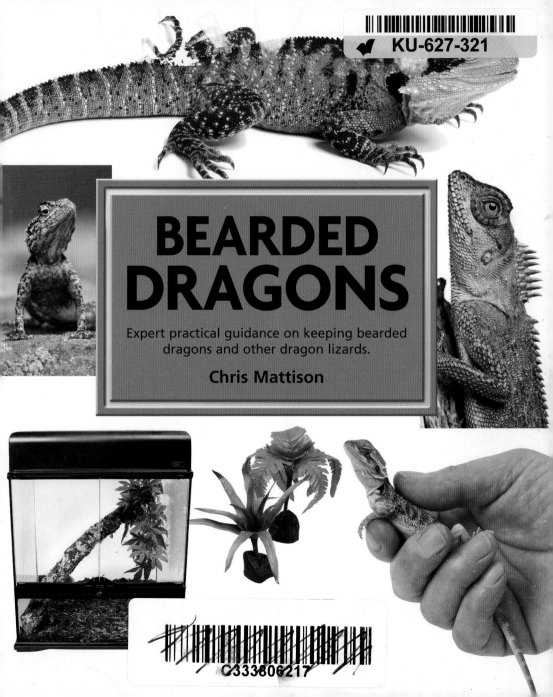

BEARDED DRAGONS

Expert practical guidance on keeping bearded dragons and other dragon lizards.

Chris Mattison

© 2011 Interpet Publishing,
Vincent Lane, Dorking, Surrey,
RH4 3YX, England.
All rights reserved.
Reprinted 2015
ISBN: 978 1 84286 232 2

Credits

Created and compiled: Ideas
into Print, Claydon, Suffolk
IP6 0AB, England.
Design and Prepress: Stuart
Watkinson, Wistaston, Cheshire
CW2 8JH, England.
Computer graphics:
Stuart Watkinson
Production management:
Consortium, Poslingford, Suffolk
CO10 8RA, England.
Print production:
1010 Printing International Ltd.

Printed and bound in China.

Chris Mattison, BSc, FRPS

Chris Mattison has an honours degree in zoology from the
University of Sheffield and specialises in the natural history
of reptiles and amphibians. He is also a Fellow of the Royal
Photographic Society and a member of several herpetological
societies. Over the years he has made many field trips to
various parts of the world, including visits to North, Central and
South America, the Galapagos Islands, southern Africa, East
Africa, South East Asia, Borneo and Madagascar, to study and
photograph reptiles and amphibians, and other wildlife.

   Chris has lectured in the UK, Sweden, Finland, Holland
and the United States on the natural history of reptiles and
amphibians and their care and breeding in
captivity. Since 1982, he has
written over 20 books and
many magazine articles
on these topics.

Contents

Part One

KEEPING DRAGON LIZARDS

Continued overleaf ▶

Contents

Part Two

SPECIES PROFILES

Hatchlings of
Uromastyx ocellata
huddle together.

Continued overleaf ▶

The Thai Water Dragon, an easily bred, popular forest dragon.

Above: A morph of the Inland Bearded Dragon, with enhanced yellow coloration.

Above: *A stunning male Mwanza Flat-headed Agama.*   **Right:** *The Ornate Dab Lizard will become tame.*

Contents

Part Two

2

SPECIES PROFILES

Bearded dragons are spectacular Australian members of the family Agamidae and the largest of the 'dragon lizards' routinely bred in captivity. They are freely available at a reasonable price and have become popular with pet keepers. Provided you take some sensible health precautions, they are good choices for children with an interest in the more exotic type of pet. Bearded dragons become very tame, are responsive to their owner and most will take food from the hand. Added interest comes from the many colour forms available.

Part One
KEEPING DRAGON LIZARDS

Dragon lizards in nature

Bearded dragons belong to the lizard family Agamidae, which contains over 400 species altogether. Not all the members of this family are called 'dragon lizards'; some are also called agamas, crested lizards, etc. However, to make it easier to generalise, we will use 'dragon lizards' for all members of the family.

Habitats

Dragon lizards live in a variety of habitats in Africa, Asia and Australasia and one species, the Starred Agama (*Laudakia stellio*) just manages to get into extreme southeast Europe. They are absent from Madagascar, North and South America and most of Europe. They include desert species, forest species, species that live among rocks and others that are at home near water.

Appearance

Dragon lizards vary in size from the smallest – the Gravel Dragon (*Cryptagama aurita*) from Australia (formerly *Tympanocryptis aurita*), which measures a maximum of 46mm snout-vent length (SVL) – to the large Sailfin Lizard (*Hydrosaurus amboinensis*) which can grow to 350mm SVL. The two largest bearded dragons – *Pogona barbata* and *P. vitticeps* – have a maximum size of 250mm SVL.

Dragon lizards are showy, diurnal (day-active) lizards. Males of some species have crests of enlarged, toothlike scales running down the centre of their backs and they may also have spines, dewlaps or frills on their chin, designed to make them look bigger to predators and rivals, and more attractive to the opposite sex.

HOW BIG DO THEY GROW?

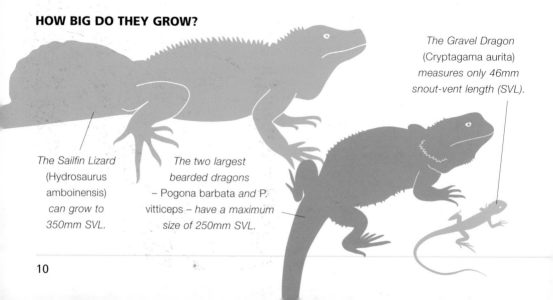

The Gravel Dragon (Cryptagama aurita) measures only 46mm snout-vent length (SVL).

The Sailfin Lizard (Hydrosaurus amboinensis) can grow to 350mm SVL.

The two largest bearded dragons – Pogona barbata and P. vitticeps – have a maximum size of 250mm SVL.

WHERE DO THEY LIVE?

The deserts of North Africa and the Middle East are home to dab lizards (Uromastyx *species*).

The tropical rainforests of Southeast Asia and the Indian sub-continent are home to most of the forest and water dragon species.

Dry grasslands in Africa are the main habitats of the Agama *species and related genera.*

Australia is home to the bearded dragons, frilled lizard and other dragon species.

Females also have crests, but they are not as well developed as those of males. Similarly, males are often more colourful than females. Unfortunately, there is little or no significant difference between the two sexes in bearded dragons or in some other species, including the dab lizards *(Uromastyx)*. In all species, the secondary sex characteristics do not begin to show until the lizard approaches sexual maturity.

Behaviour

Dragon lizards living in open habitats, such as deserts, rock outcrops, grasslands and scrub, typically perch on a prominent rock, branch or stump when they are displaying or when they are scanning for food or predators. They display to each other by bobbing their heads, doing push-ups or waving their forelimbs. Some species have brightly coloured undersides that are only visible when they push up the front of their bodies. Despite their often large size, some of the forest dragons are remarkably well camouflaged and their strategy is to cling to a sapling, vine or tree-trunk in a vertical position and remain motionless. This makes them hard to find but, at the same time, they are able to keep an eye on their surroundings. A few of the

Below: *A juvenile bearded dragon* (Pogona vitticeps) *eating a locust nymph. Young bearded dragons have hearty appetites and grow quickly.*

smaller ground-dwelling species have markings that match the sand or gravel on which they live.

All species have well-developed legs, run quickly and climb well. Some species raise the front of their body when running fast and just use their hind legs. This is known as 'bipedal' locomotion. Dragon lizards that find themselves cornered by a predator have a variety of defensive displays. They may inflate their bodies with air to make themselves look larger and more fierce. The frilled dragon erects a large ruff of skin on its neck for the same reason, while the bearded dragons puff out their throats, causing the pointed scales to stand on end. The 'beard' is often a different colour – black, for example – from the rest of their body to enhance the effect. Bearded dragons and frilled lizards rarely display in captivity.

Diet

Most dragon lizards are insectivorous, eating insects and other invertebrates, but some of the larger species also eat small vertebrates, such as rodents and other reptiles. A few are herbivores; large species may start life as insectivorous juveniles and gradually switch to a diet that includes vegetation as they grow larger. Small lizards can usually find enough insects to fill themselves up, whereas larger individuals may need to eat leaves and flowers to bulk out their diet. One group of agamids, the dab lizards, or *Uromastyx* species, are out-and-out herbivores and eat only vegetation.

How to measure a lizard

The most accurate way to measure a lizard is with a sliding calliper or a pair of dividers. Get an assistant to hold the lizard straight and upside down and place one point of the calliper or dividers in line with the tip of its snout and the other in line with its vent. This will give you the snout-vent length, usually abbreviated to SVL, which can be useful when assessing whether the lizard is breeding size, for instance. The SVL is usually preferred to the total length (TL) because lizards' tails are often damaged, regrown or deformed, introducing an element of inaccuracy. Similarly, the metric system is usually preferred, and is invariably used in scientific literature.

Measuring snout-to-vent length (SVL) is a reliable way to record size.

Breeding

All species of agamids lay eggs, with the exception of the 41 species of toad-headed lizards (*Phrynocephalus*), all of which give birth to live young. (Toad-headed lizards are from the Middle East and, though interesting, are difficult to keep in captivity and rarely available in the pet trade.) Mating and egg-laying is seasonal in species that come from temperate regions, such as southern Africa and the cooler parts of Australia, with most reproductive activity taking place in the spring and summer. However, species from tropical regions may breed at almost any time of the year. The Australian bearded dragons (*Pogona*), which are the main subject of this book, have an extended breeding season throughout the warmer months of the year but 'take a rest' during the winter. It is likely that day-length rather than temperature is responsible for controlling the breeding activity of these and the other seasonal breeders.

Australasian species

Australia and neighbouring islands such as New Guinea have a wide variety of agamids. There are 70 in Australia, mostly from the drier parts of the continent. Six of these are bearded dragons (*Pogona* species), of which three, *Pogona barbata, P. henrylawsoni* and *P. vitticeps*, are sometimes available through the pet trade. The other three are the Small-scaled Bearded Dragon (*P. microlepidota*), the Dwarf Bearded Dragon (*P. minor*) and the Nullabor Bearded

Dragon (*P. nullabor*). Another large species, the Frilled Dragon (*Chlamydosaurus kingii*), is also a popular pet species, but the majority of specimens offered for sale will have been bred from stock that originated in New Guinea, where it also occurs. Australian reptiles are protected by law so any Australian stock must be captive-bred (or has been illegally imported). Other Australian species of dragon lizards are smaller and rarely seen in the pet trade, although the Earless Lizard (*Tympanocryptis tetraporophora*) has a small following. It is rather like a juvenile bearded dragon but has more colourful markings, which camouflage it well when it is in its natural dry, rocky habitat. The Australian Water Dragon (*Physignathus lesueurii*) is seen very rarely in captivity, although its Asian cousin, the Thai Water Dragon, is much more popular.

Other species worthy of note, even though they are not available through the pet trade, are the large and spectacular Boyd's Forest Dragon (*Hypsilurus boydii*) and the Southern Angle-headed Dragon (*H. spinipes*), both of which are arboreal species that live in the rainforests along the eastern coast of Australia. Finally, the unique Thorny Devil (*Moloch horridus*) is one of the most charismatic Australian lizards, being slow-moving and covered with long thorny spines on its head, back, limbs and tail.

Right: *Boyd's Forest Dragon* (Hypsilurus boydii) *is a handsome Australian species but rarely, if ever, available through the pet trade.*

It is a desert species from Central Australia that feeds exclusively on small black ants. Not a good choice for a pet, therefore, even if it were available.

Asian and Middle-eastern species

Asian agamids include a few large, impressive species, as well as a number of smaller, inconspicuous ones.

LARGER SPECIES

Of the more showy members of the family, the Thai Water Dragon *(Physignathus cocincinus)* is the best known and is widely kept and bred in captivity. This species is semi-aquatic and closely parallels the South American Basilisk, or Jesus Christ lizards, *(Basiliscus)*, famous for their ability to run across the surface of water. Other attractive and interesting species

Right: *The Thai Water Dragon is an elegant lizard that lives alongside rivers from India to Thailand and southern China.*

Above: *A Starred Agama (Laudakia stellio) photographed on the Greek island of Kos. Up to 200mm SVL, these lizards are commonly seen there on rocks and dry stone walls.*

Right: *A male Common Garden Lizard* (Calotes versicolor) *in breeding coloration.*

include the pricklenape dragons *(Acanthosaura)*, the forest dragons *(Gonocephalus)*, garden lizards *(Calotes* and *Bronchocela)* and the spectacular Humpnosed Dragon *(Lyriocephalus scutatus)* from Sri Lanka.

SMALLER SPECIES

Smaller species include the strange and rare leafnosed dragons *(Ceratophora)*, also from Sri Lanka, a large number of Middle-eastern species, such as the rock agamas *(Laudakia* and *Trapelus)* and the toad-headed agamas *(Phrynocephalus)*. A small number of these species are sometimes available through the pet trade and notes on caring for them are given later in the book, but some are very rare. Similarly, the flying lizards *(Draco)* are occasionally imported into Europe and North America, but their requirements in captivity can rarely be met and they are usually shortlived. These lizards have large flaps of skin stretched between their elongated ribs and they use these 'wings' to glide from the trunk of one tall tree to another in the more open rainforests of Southeast Asia, including Borneo and the Philippines.

DAB LIZARDS AND BUTTERFLY LIZARDS

The dab lizards *(Uromastyx)* occur throughout the Arabian Peninsula and into the Middle East and Central Asia. A few species also occur in North Africa. Together with the seven species of butterfly lizards, they belong to a different subfamily, the Leiolepinae. Some scientists

prefer to treat them as a separate family, the Leiolepidae. The dab lizards, of which there are 14 species, are unusual in being herbivores, eating a wide variety of leaves, flowers and even twigs. They have short heads with blunt snouts and look like tortoises without shells. A number of species are available through the pet trade and some are bred in captivity. In the wild, all species lay their eggs in the female's burrow and the young remain there for several weeks after they hatch. However, the butterfly lizards *(Leiolepis)* are rarely available and usually fare poorly in captivity on the odd occasion when they are imported. The most common species is probably Bell's Butterfly Lizard *(L. belliana)* but others have been imported recently. Of the seven species in the genus, three are parthenogenetic: they are female-only species that lay viable eggs without the need to mate with a male. (There are other parthenogenetic lizards, but not in the Agamidae as far as is known, and there is at least one species of parthenogenetic snake, the Flowerpot Snake, or Brahminy Blind Snake *(Ramphotyphlops braminus.)*

African species

The most important African members of the Agamidae are the agamas, or rainbow lizards,

Left: Geyr's Dab Lizard (Uromastyx geyri) *is similar to the Spiny-tailed Dab Lizard to which it is closely related. Both species are equally suitable for captivity but their care is not always straightforward.*

belonging to the genus *Agama*, and a few other, closely related genera. These are the brilliantly coloured lizards commonly seen scampering over rocks and gravel in East and southern Africa, although they have a continent-wide range between them. Males are more brightly coloured than females and the dominant male is the brightest of all. They may have bright blue, red or pink heads and display from prominent, raised positions, bobbing their heads up and down and raising the front of their bodies by doing push-ups. Many have metallic blue undersides, which are only on show during the displays, as these are intended to warn off other males and to attract females, whose colours are duller. There are 37 species of rock and ground agamas in the genus *Agama*; some are common and wide-ranging, others have only a limited range. There are another eight or nine species of tree agamas, *Acanthocercus*. A few members of the predominantly Middle-eastern genera *Laudakia* and *Trapelus* also range into North Africa.

Right: *Male* Agama *species often have brightly coloured throats and chests. This Southern Rock Agama (*Agama atra*) is displaying to the photographer in the Karoo National Park, South Africa.*

Distant relatives

The dragon lizards are part of a larger group, or sub-order, of lizards known as the Iguania. This sub-order contains: the Agamidae, the family to which the dragon lizards belong; the Chamaeleonidae, or chameleons; the Iguanidae, or iguanas; and seven families of smaller species that are closely related to the iguanas and used to be classified with them.

The Iguania, then, is made up of a total of ten families and members of this sub-order are considered to be the most primitive living lizards. They are the direct descendents of lizards that appeared before the ancestors of all the other families, such as the geckos, skinks and monitors, for instance.

Iguanas

The iguanas and their relatives are similar in many respects to the dragon lizards: they do not occur together and one family takes the place of the other in their respective ranges. There are many examples where a species of agama looks

THE IGUANIA GROUP

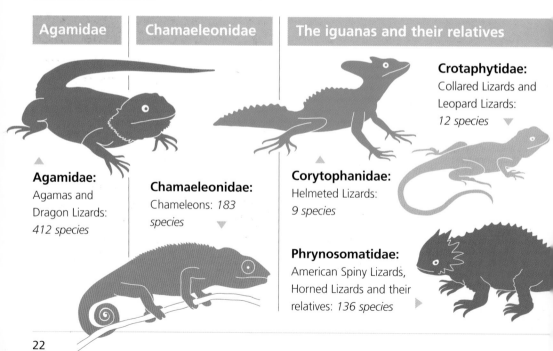

Agamidae	Chamaeleonidae	The iguanas and their relatives

Agamidae:
Agamas and
Dragon Lizards:
412 species

Chamaeleonidae:
Chameleons: *183 species*

Crotaphytidae:
Collared Lizards and
Leopard Lizards:
12 species

Corytophanidae:
Helmeted Lizards:
9 species

Phrynosomatidae:
American Spiny Lizards,
Horned Lizards and their
relatives: *136 species*

and behaves in a similar fashion to a species of iguana, even though they are in different families and live on different continents. For example, the water dragons *(Physignathus)* – members of the Agamidae from Asia and Australia – are almost indistinguishable to a non-herpetologist (see the panel on herpetology) from the basilisks *(Basiliscus species)*, which are members of the Corytophanidae, part of the 'old' Iguanidae, from Central America. This is an example of convergent evolution and there are several other examples between the two families.

Iguanas occur in North and South America, the West Indies, Galapagos Islands, Madagascar and Fiji. There are rather more iguanids than there are agamids and they are more varied. There are 1006 species grouped under the eight families that make up the 'iguanas', compared to the 412 species of agamids. The very large genus *Anolis* accounts for 376 of the iguana species.

LARGE AND MEDIUM-SIZED IGUANAS

The Green Iguana *(Iguana iguana)* is the best-known member of its group of families. It is a large, arboreal, green or greenish lizard, with an impressive crest along its back and large dewlaps that flap about when it nods its head in display. This species, like many of the other large iguanids, is a herbivore. One of its close relatives is the Marine Iguana *(Amblyrhynchus*

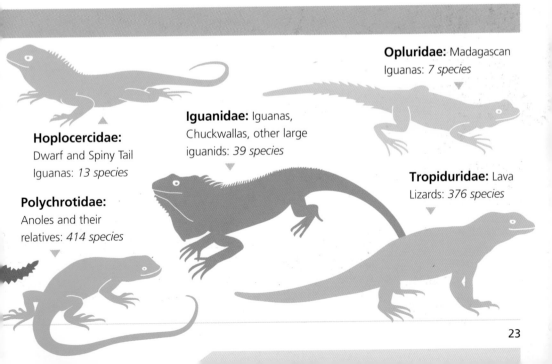

Opluridae: Madagascan Iguanas: *7 species*

Hoplocercidae: Dwarf and Spiny Tail Iguanas: *13 species*

Iguanidae: Iguanas, Chuckwallas, other large iguanids: *39 species*

Tropiduridae: Lava Lizards: *376 species*

Polychrotidae: Anoles and their relatives: *414 species*

Above: The Green Iguana (Iguana iguana) is one of the most familiar lizard species and has a wide range over much of Central and South America. It is a close relative of the dragon lizards but belongs to the Iguanidae.

cristatus) from the Galapagos Islands, the only ocean-going lizard and the only one that eats seaweed. Rhinoceros Iguanas *(Cyclura* spp.) occur on a number of islands in the West Indies and are large, impressive and threatened with extinction by the destruction of their habitats and introduced predators, such as dogs. The Chuckwallas *(Sauromalus* spp.) are heavily built iguanids from North America that live on rock outcrops, jamming themselves into crevices by inflating their bodies if a predator tries to catch them. They, too, are herbivores, eating succulent plants, including cacti. The Desert Iguana *(Dipsosaurus dorsalis)* is a medium-sized species from North America that has been bred in captivity on a small scale. It is also a herbivore and makes a good captive if given plenty of heat and light. Collared and Leopard lizards *(Crotaphytus* spp.) have large heads. These are colourful predatory species, some of which are also bred in captivity.

SMALLER IGUANAS

Of the many smaller species allied to the iguanas, the anoles are often seen in the pet trade, especially the Green Anole *(Anolis carolinensis)* from North America. Other species come from Cuba and the West Indies. Several have been introduced into Florida and these are also available occasionally. Anolis lizards are good climbers and live in shrubs and on tree trunks. Some species have adapted to human activities and are common around houses and buildings.

What is herpetology?

Herpetology is the study of reptiles and amphibians. Although these two groups are not especially closely related to one other (in fact, reptiles are more closely related to birds than they are to amphibians) they have traditionally been studied together, partly because they tend to live in similar places and because the techniques for finding and collecting them are often similar. The term comes from a Greek word 'herpeton' meaning a creeping animal. Reptiles and amphibians are sometimes referred to as 'herptiles', which is a made-up word, as is its shorter version 'herps'. People who study and are interested in reptiles and amphibians are known as herpetologists, whether they are professional scientists or amateur hobbyists, while some people refer to keepers and breeders of reptiles and amphibians as 'herpetoculturalists'.

The American Spiny Lizards, or Swifts, *(Sceloporus* species) are common in North and Central America and fare quite well in captivity, provided they are given enough warmth but, unfortunately, captive-bred animals are rarely available. The Horned Lizards *(Phrynosoma* spp.) are among the most interesting species. They eat mostly ants, consuming several hundreds

What is convergent evolution?

Animals from different parts of the world that live in similar environments sometimes evolve along similar lines as a result of the conditions they find there, resulting in pairs or groups of species that look and behave in the same way, even though they are not related. This is known as convergent evolution. Emus and ostriches are one such example and, among reptiles, the Green Tree Python and the Emerald Tree Boa are so similar that they can easily be mistaken for one another. Examples also occur among iguanids and agamids. The American Chuckwallas (Sauromalus

Above: Townsend's Chuckwalla (Sauromalus obesus townsendi), a member of the Iguanidae from northern Mexico, lives on rocky hillsides.

Below: The habitat and lifestyle of the Eyed Dab Lizard (Uromastyx ocellata), a North African agamid, are similar to the Chuckwalla's, so the two species have come to look like each other.

species), which belong to the Iguanidae, and the North African and Middle Eastern Dab Lizards (Uromastyx species), which are members of the Agamidae, are similar to each other in their appearance and in many other respects. Both groups of species are predominantly herbivorous as adults and live in burrows or rock crevices in dry, arid places. They are stocky lizards with thick tails that store fat and are used to block the lizards' burrows from pursuing predators. The lizards can also inflate their bodies, making them more difficult to dislodge when they are wedged into a crevice.

in a single session, by sitting next to a trail and picking off the ants one by one as they pass by. They are short and squat with short legs, and run for only short distances, relying on their camouflage to escape detection. Because of their specialised diet, they do not fare well in captivity and should not be caught or purchased.

Chameleons

Chameleons, which occur in Africa, Madagascar and southern Asia, are highly specialised and very distinct from any other lizards; anybody should be able to recognise a chameleon. It can be hard to believe that they are the dragon lizards' and iguanids' closest relatives.

Chameleons are attractive and charismatic lizards. Most species are arboreal and all

Below: *The Painted Swift* (Liolaemus pictus) *from Chile is a member of the Tropiduridae (closely related to the Iguanidae). This large genus occurs over much of the South American Andes.*

their adaptations – their leaflike shape, green coloration, independently swivelling eyes, pincerlike feet and prehensile tail – are associated with this lifestyle. Although chameleons are famous for the colour-changing abilities, these are often exaggerated. A few chameleons live on the ground, including a number of small brown species in the genera *Rhampholeon*, the Leaf Chameleons of Africa, and *Brookesia*, the Dwarf Chameleons of Madagascar. *Brookesia minima* is one of the world's smallest lizards.

An unusual chameleon from the Namib Desert *(Chamaeleo namaquensis)* looks like an arboreal species, but lives far from any forests, feeding on beetles that live among sand dunes. Large, showy species include the Panther Chameleon *(Furcifer pardalis)*, Parson's Chameleon *(Furcifer parsonii),* the Veiled, or Yemen, Chameleon *(Chamaeleo calyptratus)* from the Arabian Peninsula, and Jackson's, or Three-horned Chameleon *(Chamaeleo jacksonii)* from East Africa.

Keeping chameleons in captivity is not easy but some species, such as the Panther Chameleon and Veiled Chameleon, are being bred very successfully. If you are tempted to buy chameleons, you are strongly recommended to buy captive-bred animals. If possible, buy directly from the breeder, who will also be able to supply information on the way they have been kept.

Right: *A colourful form of the Panther Chameleon* (Furcifer pardalis) *from Ambilobe, Madagascar.*

Choosing dragon lizards

In the last decade or so, reptiles have become much more acceptable as 'pets'. This is because equipment and techniques have improved enormously and, at the same time, there is now a better understanding of the animals' environmental and nutritional needs. As a result, there is a good selection of captive-bred animals, and the equipment and knowledge-base necessary to keep them healthy is readily available. A number of species of snakes and lizards are now common in captivity and at a reasonable price, all produced by a small army of hobbyists and commercial breeders.

Bearded dragons are one of the two most popular lizard species, the other one being the leopard gecko. In addition, there are dedicated breeders putting their efforts into a wide range of other species, such as water dragons, frilled lizards, panther chameleons and several more. Any of these species is worth considering when choosing a lizard, but the bearded dragon is probably the one with the greatest following for a number of reasons.

Why choose a bearded dragon?

The bearded dragon is large (but not too large), attractive, adapts well to captivity, is responsive, does not bite and is relatively easy to house and care for. With a little extra attention it will also breed in captivity, giving its keeper the pleasure of seeing the whole life-cycle unfold before their eyes. If there is a downside to keeping bearded dragons it is that they require large enclosures. This is something you need to consider carefully when buying a bearded dragon. The problem will not magically go away; indeed, as the lizard grows, so will the problem. Baby bearded dragons are cute, but adults are bulky, boisterous and active. They need plenty of space. If this is likely to be a problem they are best avoided and a leopard gecko (or a stick insect!) would be a better choice.

Which kind of bearded dragon?

Having decided that you do have the space to keep one or more bearded dragons, the next question is 'Which kind?' Beginners should always choose the Inland, or Central, Bearded Dragon (Pogona vitticeps). It is by far the most common species because it is the one that

Right: Choosing a healthy bearded dragon in the first place is an important step towards keeping it successfully. Look at several and decide whether to start out with a juvenile or adult. Staff in pet stores should be able to provide basic information on whether the lizards are feeding properly and what food they prefer. Do not be in too much of a hurry to buy your dragon. Set up the vivarium first and make sure the temperature and lighting equipment are both working properly before bringing the dragon to its new home.

adapts best to captivity. The other species are for specialists.

The next decision is whether to buy one of the colour forms (often known in the hobby as 'morphs') that have arisen, some from strains of wild-caught animals that are particularly colourful and some that have cropped up in captivity. Many of these unusually coloured individuals have been selectively bred, producing a kaleidoscope of different strains, and breeders are producing new forms all the time. Some are attractive, others less so, and yet others are so similar to the wild type that paying a premium for them seems a waste of money. Ultimately, only you can decide: beauty, as always, is in the eye of the beholder. Remember that, in general, selectively bred animals can be weaker than normal stock as they are often inbred. Inbreeding is not necessarily a bad thing, just something to bear in mind. If you do choose one of the colour forms, try to see the parents from whence it came. Juvenile bearded dragons tend to be similar to each other, regardless of which form they are, and the adult colours do not show in their full glory until they approach maturity.

Which one to buy?

The next decision – the best part – is choosing which individual or individuals to buy. The most readily available bearded dragons will be captive-bred juveniles. Hatchlings just out of the egg are not ideal choices; they are delicate, may not have started to feed regularly and will show little

Bearded dragons available in the pet trade

Over the years, a number of bearded dragons have been available through the pet trade. Apart from the Inland Bearded Dragon (Pogona vitticeps), *which is the species most often offered for sale, two other bearded dragons, the Rankin's Bearded Dragon and the Eastern Bearded Dragon* (Pogona henrylawsoni and P. barbata), *are sometimes bred in captivity. In addition, some of the bearded dragons offered for sale are hybrids between Rankin's Bearded Dragon and the Inland Bearded Dragon. There is no doubt that the best bearded dragon for beginners is the Inland Bearded Dragon and the other species should be left to the experts.*

or none of their potential colour. By the time they are about a month old, bearded dragons should measure about 20cm in total length and this is the best size at which to buy them. Whether you buy from a pet shop or a breeder, the young bearded dragons will almost certainly be in a group of similarly sized individuals and you should be able to see which are the most active and healthy.

Look for an individual that basks and has an alert, upright stance. Its eyes should be wide open and bright. Well-fed individuals have a plump base to their tail. If you can persuade the seller to feed the lizards while you are watching, you will see which are the most assertive and dominant individuals – these are the ones to buy. Any that sulk in a corner, have closed or sunken eyes, skinny limbs and tail, or any signs of physical damage should be avoided. If there are more than one or two in this condition it is often a good idea to walk away and find another source. Although bearded dragons are tough, even as juveniles, they do occasionally suffer from nutritional problems, diseases and parasites and it is important to avoid these.

WHAT TO LOOK OUT FOR

The base of the tail should be plump. If there are signs of bones showing, the lizard has probably not been feeding enough.

Tail tips may become broken through fighting or if they are trapped in a cage door. This is not usually serious but the tail will not regrow.

Both eyes should be bright and clear. Dull eyes could indicate an infection or general lack of condition.

Lizard should be alert and have a good posture, with its head and front part of its body raised.

Lizards that have not shed properly sometimes lose the tips of their toes. Although not necessarily a serious problem it can indicate that conditions have not been ideal.

How many to buy?

Buying a pair or small group of bearded dragons at the outset can be an attractive proposition. They will interact with each other as they grow up and, although this can sometimes lead to one becoming dominant over the other, once a pecking order has been established there will be little or no conflict between them. The extra cost of keeping two bearded dragons rather than a single one is not great after the initial cost of purchase. They will live together in the same cage, the costs of heating and lighting will obviously be the same and the extra food bill will be negligible. If you think you will eventually want to breed bearded dragons then it goes without saying that you will need a pair or a small group – many breeders keep one male with two females – in which case it is better to buy them together when they are juveniles and let them grow up together as a social unit. This, of course, presupposes

that you, or the dealer/breeder, can determine their sexes at a fairly young age, and this is not always obvious. (For advice on sexing bearded dragons, see *Breeding* pages 94-96).

If, on the other hand, you decide to keep a single bearded dragon, it may make a more responsive pet and will react to you in the same way that it would react to other bearded dragons: head-bobbing and arm-waving are methods of communication that will be redirected at the keeper in the absence of other individuals of the same species. Again, only you can decide if this is a good thing or not.

Buying larger bearded dragons

Occasionally, you will see larger bearded dragons for sale. They might be adults that are surplus

Below: Bearded dragons of a few days old are lively, engaging creatures. Choosing which one(s) to buy can be difficult, but avoid any that seem less active than the others.

Above: *At eight months old bearded dragons should have settled into their new home and become tame and easy to handle.*

to a breeding colony or half-grown individuals that become available when a breeder 'thins out' his colony. This can be a good way of obtaining quality animals without having

to wait for them to grow, but you still need to follow the precautions regarding health.

Quarantining new stock

If you already have one or more bearded dragons and have bought another to add to your group, it is essential to quarantine it first. Keep it in a separate cage, and preferably in a separate room. Feed it, clean it and handle it after you have attended to your established animals and

35

use a separate set of scoops, food bowls and so on. Wash your hands with a disinfectant wash after any contact with the dragon or its cage furnishings. Check its faeces and if they look at all suspicious – loose or an unusual colour – get them screened for diseases or parasites. Only when you are 100% certain that the new animal is in the clear should you consider introducing it to an established group. This is achieved when there are no outward signs of ill-health and after at least two successive faecal samples, taken a week apart, come back from the veterinarian or laboratory with no signs of infection.

Introducing new stock

The next stage is getting the new animal and the established one(s) to accept each other. A new pecking order will have to be established and this can lead to stress. The amount of stress will depend on what sex they are, whether they are mature and whether there is any difference in size. You will have to watch the animals carefully and if there are signs of serious fighting or injury, remove the new individual. In any case, it is a bad idea to introduce a lizard that differs significantly in size from the established ones.

Other species

Buying other species of dragon lizards follows much the same course as for bearded dragons, except that very few captive-bred examples will be available. Apart from bearded dragons, Thai Water Dragons and some of the dab lizards are bred in captivity in sufficient numbers to enter the pet trade. Other species can appear on the market

Left: An alert young Thai Water Dragon (Physignathus cocincinus) *This captive-bred individual would be a good choice and will quickly adapt to a new home.*

Above: *The Long-tailed Earless Dragon* (Tympanocryptis tetraporophora) *is relatively new on the scene, but appears to be a good alternative to bearded dragons if you have limited space.*

occasionally, but breeders often sell or exchange them directly with friends or distribute them through the membership of a reptile society. Captive-bred animals are often more expensive than wild-caught ones and so they should be; breeding and rearing lizards is an expensive and time-consuming business. On the other hand, the chances of successfully rearing and maintaining captive-bred animals in the long term are infinitely greater.

If you cannot resist the lure of a wild-caught dragon lizard – for example, if you are attracted to one of the species that is not available captive-bred – quarantine precautions are even more important. When buying wild-caught lizards, some lizard keepers send faecal samples to a laboratory (or their veterinarian) as a matter of course, as many animals will harbour parasites. You will also need to be extra careful to select animals that look healthy, lively and in good condition. Pay special attention to the base of the tail and the limbs, which should be plump, not withered, and to the snout, which is often damaged and can become infected.

However, the very best advice is to steer clear of wild-caught animals and stick to a species that is readily available, such as one of the bearded dragons. This cannot be emphasised enough.

Handling bearded dragons

One of the attractions of bearded dragons over some other reptiles is that they can be handled easily, without stress to the lizard or the keeper. They will not bite, scratch or defaecate all over you like some other species. Young bearded dragons are quite delicate and should be handled with care. In fact, it is better to allow them to climb onto your hand than to try to pick them up. Because they have a natural tendency to climb upwards, they will see your hand and arm as a good lookout post and will often climb aboard with little encouragement. If you offer food, especially something they are particularly fond of, such as waxworms, this will encourage them even more.

Try not to grab at a lizard because this will alarm it; far better to let it come to you and grow in confidence than to force it to do

Above: *There is no need to grip tame lizards tightly. Just be ready to restrain them gently if they try to jump away.*

Below: *Bearded dragons will soon become accustomed to being handled and will happily sit on your hand.*

something it is wary of. Adult bearded dragons are tougher and less easily stressed but, even so, be careful of dropping them and, again, allow them to rest on your arm or lap rather than holding them tightly.

Sometimes you might have to hold the lizard more firmly, for sex determination or to administer a drug, for instance. In this case, the technique is to grasp it gently but firmly around the neck and forepart of the body, lift it off the ground and immediately support its abdomen and base of the tail with your other hand. If you

Below: Some other species do not tame down quite as easily and need to be restrained at first. This is a Thai Water Dragon.

Taking dragon lizards home

Transport dragon lizards in a plastic or cardboard box or, for longer journeys, a polystyrene box. Add crumpled newspaper, so that the lizards are not thrown around during the journey. Take them home immediately and do not leave them in a car. Their cage should have been set up well in advance. Although lizards may not feed straight away, you can offer a small amount of food a few hours after installing them. Watch their behaviour carefully for the first few days for any signs of stress and try not to disturb them more than necessary. Keep handling to a minimum while they settle in.

need to turn it over, change your grip slightly so that you are lightly gripping it in the region of its front and back legs. When you put it back in the enclosure, release it slowly and carefully, putting the back legs on the ground first.

Handling other species follows much the same sequence, although many of them are not as cooperative as bearded dragons. These species should be handled as little as possible – many of them can be sexed visually, for example – and, where possible, try to pick them up in the morning, before they have fully warmed up. Be aware that some agamid lizards are quite likely to bite and, in the case of the larger species, this can be quite painful.

Frilled lizards soon become tame and are willing to sit on the hand with the minimum of restraint. Just make sure that their body is well supported, otherwise they will feel insecure and struggle.

Above: *Handling an Eyed Dab Lizard* (Uromastyx ocellata) *from North Africa. Note the spiny, club-shaped tail, which the lizard can use as a weapon.*

Creating the right environment

Captive lizards are not able to move about to find the environment that suits them best, as they would in the wild. This means that you, the owner, have to provide them with the correct conditions. The environment we are concerned with here is made up of three main parameters – heat, light and humidity – and the way in which they interact. In this section we look at the equipment you will need to provide. In the following section we see how to incorporate these systems into an enclosure.

Species requirements

Taking the dragon lizards (Agamidae) as a whole, there are two distinct groups and their requirements differ greatly. Firstly, there are the species from hot, dry places that experience clear skies for many months each year. Bearded dragons are in this category, as are frilled lizards, rock agamas and ground agamas.

The other group contains the forest lizards, coming mostly from tropical regions. These lizards, which include the prickle-nape lizards, water dragons and forest dragons, live beneath the forest canopy, which evens out the extremes of temperature and light. Some radiation, in the form of infra-red, visual and ultraviolet light does get through, but not as much as in deserts and grasslands. Furthermore, the soil in these places acts like a sponge, soaking up water whenever it rains and releasing it gradually to produce

humidity the rest of the time. Even during the 'dry' season humidity levels are fairly high. Species from this type of environment should be treated appropriately, which involves spraying their enclosure by hand or by means of an automatic sprinkler system and by giving them more subdued lighting and heating. In addition, they should be provided with plenty of places to shelter, preferably living plants. Generally speaking, forest lizards are more difficult to cater for than desert ones.

Above: *Many agamids are heat- and light-loving desert species and this must be taken into account when creating a captive environment for them.*

DRY, OPEN FOREST AND SCRUB

Daily high temperature

Daily low temperature

Open eucalyptus
woodland in Australia
is the home of many
agamid lizards, including
bearded dragons and
frilled lizards.

Rainfall

Jan — One year — Dec

Typical conditions

*Rainfall is low at all
times, and conditions
are hot and dry.
However, there
are some seasonal
changes in average
temperature, with a
definite cool period
in June, July and
August.*

HUMID RAINFOREST

Daily high temperature

Daily low temperature

Closed-canopy
rainforests are the
preferred habitat of
forest dragons, such
as the Gonocephalus
species and the flying
lizards, Draco species.

Rainfall

Jan — One year — Dec

Typical conditions

*Rainfall is high
throughout the year,
with peaks during
two well-defined
rainy seasons, but
the humidity is high
at all times. However,
the temperature is
almost constant
throughout the year
and varies little from
day to night.*

Natural temperature regulation

Firstly, it is important to understand how bearded dragons and other reptiles regulate their temperatures in the wild. They are 'ectotherms', which simply means that they rely on outside sources of heat to maintain their body temperatures at the correct level. This differs from the system used by birds and mammals, including humans, which generate heat internally through the metabolism of food. Being an ectotherm is not necessarily a disadvantage. Because they do not use up energy to raise their body temperature, ectotherms can survive on much less food than birds or mammals – perhaps as little as one-tenth. This is an advantage for those species living in places such as deserts, where food is in short supply, and it is for this reason that reptiles are often the dominant form of animal life in arid regions across the world.

Ectotherms need to keep their body temperature at a fairly high level so that they can carry out all the normal bodily functions, such as locomotion, digestion, producing eggs and sperm, etc. If their body temperature falls below a certain point they slow down and cease to function properly. If it reaches a critical level, they

HOW DRAGON LIZARDS REGULATE THEIR BODY TEMPERATURE

Even within a small area, temperature can vary greatly. Lizards can shuttle between hot and cooler areas to regulate their body temperature very accurately.

Apart from moving around, lizards can regulate the amount of heat they absorb by changing their body shape and orientating it towards the sun.

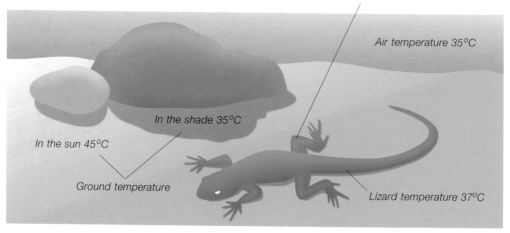

Air temperature 35°C

In the shade 35°C

In the sun 45°C

Ground temperature

Lizard temperature 37°C

Above: *Boyd's Forest Dragon lives in the rainforests of Queensland, where its environment is very different from that of the bearded dragons, which live in the arid interior.*

lose the power of movement altogether and will eventually die. Similarly, if their body temperature rises too much, they suffer heat exhaustion.

Different species have slightly different preferred body temperatures but, generally speaking, lizards try to keep their body temperatures between about 30°C and 40°C.

They do this by basking and by moving from warm places to cooler ones. In the morning they emerge and bask until their body temperature is at the preferred level, then they may go off and forage for food or interact with each other. If these activities involve a drop in temperature (if they have to move to a cooler place to find food, for instance) they will return to the basking place every so often to top up their body temperature.

Tricks for capturing as much heat as possible include flattening the body and tilting it towards the heat source. If the animal's basking place is a rock, it will also press its body onto the rock to absorb heat through its underside. Some species turn dark when they are actively absorbing heat and become paler when they reach their preferred temperature.

Heating the enclosure

In captivity, the opportunities to move around into and out of warm and cool places are more limited, but the ideal cage will allow the lizards to do this is much as possible. At one end of the cage, place overhead heating focused on a basking place, or 'hot-spot', that the animals can easily reach. If there is more than one lizard in the cage the hot-spot should be big enough for all of them. There are many types of heating lamps, some of which also give off light. Leaving aside the subject of lighting for the time being, the aim for heating is to achieve a temperature immediately under the light that is in excess of 40°C (slightly less in the case of forest species).

CREATING HOT AND COOL SPOTS

The lizard enclosure should duplicate conditions in the wild, with hot and cooler areas so that the lizard can thermoregulate naturally.

A hot-spot is very important and should be created over a pile of rocks or some other basking area.

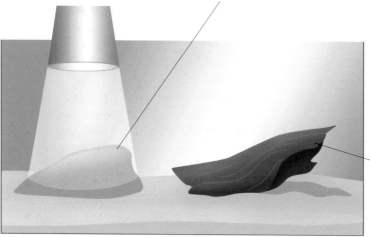

Above: *When the light first comes on, the lizards crowd together underneath it. They often climb on top of each other to get as close as possible to the heat source.*

An area of shade is equally important and this can be an overhanging rock or an artificial hide box.

This will allow the lizards to warm up quickly after the lamp is turned on and still have plenty of time for other activities.

CHOOSING A HEATER

The size of the heater you will need depends on many factors, but mainly on the background temperature and how well insulated the vivarium is. For example, heat builds up more quickly in wooden enclosures than it does in glass ones. If you buy your cage and equipment locally, the dealer should be able to advise on this, but some trial and error may still be necessary. If the heater is too powerful the lizards will not want to bask under it and this is your cue to move it further away from the basking spot or replace it with a less powerful one. Let the behaviour of the lizards be your guide.

REGULATING THE HEATING

Whether or not it also gives off light, the basking lamp should be turned on at a regular time each day and this is best regulated by using a simple time switch. This will give the lizards a day and night cycle and their behaviour will be more natural and predictable. As long as the heat source is at one end of the cage only – and the lizards can get away from it – there should be no need for a thermostat.

Because the basking lamp will be switched off at night, some form of background heating may be necessary to prevent the vivarium becoming

Above: Heat mats come in many sizes. Choose one that covers about one quarter to one half the floor area of your vivarium.

Above: This young bearded dragon has climbed to the top of its rock pile and is basking in the heat of a heat-lamp, while also absorbing UV-B rays from a separate light.

too cold. This can be an under-cage heat mat, controlled by a thermostat. The background temperature for bearded dragons and most other dragon lizards should be between 20°C and 25°C at the surface of the sand, although slightly lower temperatures will not be harmful. The heat pad does not have to cover the entire base of the vivarium but it should cover at least one-third. Again, this will give the lizards a choice of temperature.

In the wild, some forest species do not have many opportunities for basking and they probably operate at lower temperatures than desert species. Having said this, night-time temperatures in forests are not as low as those in deserts, which lose heat quickly once the sun goes down, so forest species need a more constant temperature. In captivity, background heating is more important for these species, and basking lights can be less powerful.

Choosing a thermostat

Thermostats are not all the same but come in four basic types.

Simple temperature thermostat This switches the power off when the set temperature has been reached and back on again when it has dropped by two or three degrees. It is cheap to buy and effective with apparatus such as heat mats, but is not suitable for use with light bulbs and spotlights used as basking lights because the constant switching on and off will shorten the

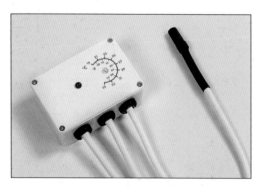

Above: *A simple on-off thermostat. Choose a thermostat that is suitable for the equipment you intend to use. Place the sensor inside the enclosure, but attach the control unit to the outside. You may have to drill a small hole in one of the sides of the vivarium.*

life of the bulb and disturb the animals. Also, if the cage is in a living room of your home, the constant flickering will become annoying, to say the least.

Dimming thermostat This gradually increases or reduces the power, resulting in a very stable temperature with no switching on or off, and is the best choice for light bulbs and spotlights, but is unsuitable for fluorescent lighting. It can also be used with heat mats and ceramic heaters.

Pulse proportional thermostat

This produces controlled pulses of power and is recommended for ceramic heaters but not lights.

Day and night thermostat

This can be of the dimming type or the pulse proportional type. It is used to set a temperature drop of up to about 15°C for a predetermined time at night, giving a natural cycle automatically.

You should not rely solely on the thermostat's scale when setting the temperature. Use a separate thermometer, preferably a digital one with a remote sensor and maximum and minimum settings. When first establishing the temperature in a vivarium, take readings from several different places. If necessary, fine tune the temperature by using the thermostat.

In a large enclosure, installed in a room with a background temperature of 15°C or more, you

Above: A thermometer made for aquariums but equally suitable for vivariums. This model gives readings for inside and outside the vivarium and can also be set to record the minimum and maximum temperatures over a period of time. This inexpensive piece of equipment is extremely useful when setting up a vivarium and for monitoring it on a permanent basis.

spotlights or if they are positioned near a window. In this case, thermostats are necessary to stop them from overheating. As every situation is different, it is not possible to give hard and fast rules and a degree of common sense has to used.

When buying electrical equipment of any type, but especially equipment for heating the vivarium, seek advice from the retailer because factors such as the size of the vivarium, type of heater, background temperature in your home, and so on, will influence your final set-up. Follow the manufacturers' instructions carefully.

Above: A dimming vivarium thermostat, probably the best choice for an enclosure housing bearded dragons and similar species.

may not need a thermostat at all. The basking lamp can be controlled by a simple time-switch, along with the lighting, and the heat mat can be left on permanently. The vivarium temperature will fall at night but this is natural, and the lizards will be able to chose their preferred temperature by moving about from one end of the vivarium to the other if the heat mat is placed at one end only, as recommended.

On the other hand, small enclosures have a tendency to overheat if they have powerful

Lighting the enclosure

In the case of day-active lizards, such as bearded dragons, lighting serves more than one purpose. Firstly, visible light allows them to see things. This is pretty obvious, but bearded dragons, in particular, come from a part of the world where skies are clear and the sun is intense, especially in the middle part of the day. As a result, they have a psychological need for bright conditions. In addition, lizards' eyes are more sensitive to the violet end of the spectrum than the eyes of humans, so they see colours slightly differently. Finding food might be affected by the way in which their enclosure is lit and, although it is difficult to know how important this is to the animals, it seems sensible to supply light that includes wavelengths in the ultraviolet range.

ULTRAVIOLET LIGHT

Ultraviolet light is divided into two types, depending on its wavelength. Ultraviolet A, or

UV-A, has a long wavelength, between 320 and 400 nanometres (nm). This is the wavelength that lizards can see, but humans cannot, so they see colours and patterns that are invisible to us. The other type is ultraviolet B, or UV-B, which has a shorter wavelength, between 290 and 320nm. Light of this type is vitally important to many lizards, including bearded dragons and all other agamids. Without it they cannot synthesise Vitamin D_3 and, without Vitamin D_3, they cannot absorb calcium into their systems. So, even if they have access to calcium, without access to UV-B as well they cannot use it and will still suffer deficiencies.

Calcium is important in the transmission of nerve impulses and in building bones. Symptoms of calcium deficiency include general lethargy, poor muscle tone and a weak skeleton. It is sometimes known as metabolic bone disease (MBD). Herbivorous reptiles, such as dab lizards and adult bearded dragons, are especially

HEAT AND LIGHT OPTIONS

Lighting is vitally important. There is a great variety of equipment available, so study the options and seek advice from the supplier about specific makes and models.

Linear UV-B tube or spiral

Mercury vapour lamp

UV-B	UV-A	VISIBLE
290	320	400

vulnerable, as are growing youngsters of all species and females that are producing eggs. For more information on this important subject see *Feeding* (page 82), *Health* (pages 88-90) and *Breeding* (page 99).

INFRA-RED LIGHT

Light from the other end of the spectrum, the infra-red end, is transmitted as heat. Wavelengths of this type are generated by incandescent lights. Their energy is given off mainly as heat, with some light as well, by lamps with a red filter that excludes most of the visible light, and by ceramic heaters that provide heat but do not give out any light at all. Rays from this end of the spectrum are absorbed by basking lizards to raise their body temperatures.

Under natural conditions, lizards bask in the sun to get warm and absorb UV-B at the same time. In captivity, most keepers are not able to provide enough natural sunshine and

have to use artificial sources. There are several approaches.

MERCURY VAPOUR LAMPS

There are lights on the market that produce heat, visible light, UV-A and UV-B radiation from a single source. They are known as mercury vapour lamps. Products designed specifically for reptiles are ideal. A single lamp can be directed onto the cage's hot-spot and the lizards will enjoy high levels of UV-A and UV-B as they bask in the heat. This closely replicates the way they behave in the wild. Perfect! Unfortunately, there are drawbacks. Although mercury vapour lamps are available in different power ratings, they all give out high levels of radiation, including heat, whenever they are on and they cannot be regulated by thermostats or dimmers. This means that they should be positioned at least 45cm above the basking rock and are therefore only suitable for very large enclosures and, preferably,

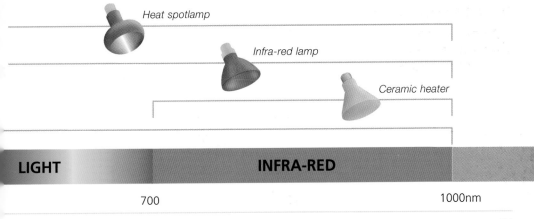

Heat spotlamp

Infra-red lamp

Ceramic heater

LIGHT

INFRA-RED

700

1000nm

ones with open or mesh tops, so that the lamp(s) can be suspended above them and outside the cage itself. They are also expensive, although prices have fallen recently. However, if you have a large enough cage – and deep pockets – they are the most elegant answer to the problem of lighting and heating.

HALOGEN PLUS FLUORESCENT LAMPS

There are other ways of providing the right types and amount of light. Halogen lamps, in the form of spotlights, can be used to provide heat and visible light. There are many types of these, some of them giving out slightly different spectrums of light. There are even dark blue versions that

Above: This bearded dragon is enjoying the heat produced from a simple spotlight. If a UV-B tube is positioned nearby, it will also benefit from its rays while it is basking.

simulate moonlight while still providing a small amount of heat. In common with the mercury-vapour lamps, halogen lamps are directed onto the basking rock to create a hot-spot (page 46).

The UV-B is then produced by a separate unit, usually a special UV-B fluorescent lamp, mounted alongside the heat lamp. These are available as straight (linear) tubes or as spirals. Spirals are more compact and suitable for small vivariums, such as those housing, for example, juveniles or smaller species. These lamps are available in several power ratings, each producing a different amount of UV light. A lamp giving 5% UV-B is often recommended for young bearded dragons and forest species. However, as the UV-B rays fall off quite rapidly with distance, a 10% UV-B lamp may be needed for tall cages, where the lizards are not able to approach the light source very closely. Ideally, they should be positioned no more than 30cm from the lizards' basking place.

There are also lamps that give out lower amounts of UV-B but these are not suitable for day-active, basking species unless they are mounted side-by-side with a lamp producing a higher dose of UV-B. They are sometimes known as 'full-spectrum' lamps because they give out a balanced light that includes all visible wavelengths and are ideal for the benefit of the viewer and for plant growth.

REPLACING LAMPS

Note that the UV-B emission of all fluorescent lamps decreases over time. After one year, they

Heating and lighting options

It is clear that heating and lighting often go hand-in-hand. The method(s) you opt for will depend on the size of the cage and the size of your pocket. Whichever you choose, you will need an under-cage heat pad to provide a background temperature of about 20-25°C over part of the cage floor, preferably controlled by a thermostat, and a time-switch to control the lighting. In summary, here are the options:

Option 1

A mercury-vapour lamp, which will provide heat and light in the correct wavelengths. Make sure it is focused on a pile of rocks or basking spot at one end of the cage so that the lizards can get away from it.

***Advantages** Convenient, natural.*
***Disadvantages** Expensive; too powerful for small set-ups.*

Use mercury vapour lamps with care, as their output cannot be effectively controlled by a thermostat and they are too powerful for small enclosures.

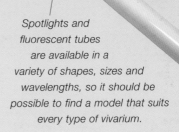

Spotlights and fluorescent tubes are available in a variety of shapes, sizes and wavelengths, so it should be possible to find a model that suits every type of vivarium.

Option 2

An incandescent, infra-red light or halogen lamp or spotlight to provide heat and one or more separate lamps for the visual and UV-B wavelengths. These can be linear fluorescent tubes or more compact spirals. If you take this option, make sure the fluorescent lamps give out enough UV-B and change them regularly.

***Advantages** Inexpensive; wide range of wattages available for both heating and lighting so useful for cages of all sizes.*
***Disadvantages** More than one unit to fit and wire in.*

give off only about 50% of the UV-B that they do when new, assuming they are on for 12 hours each day. This means that, although they continue to give off visible light, they need to be changed regularly. If you use two lamps in the cage you can stagger the dates you change them, so that one new lamp is installed every six months.

LIGHT CYCLES

Light cycles are important for natural behaviour. In nature, the day length varies throughout the year except on the equator. If you use a time switch to control the heating and lighting you can make small changes throughout the year to simulate this. Twelve hours on and 12 hours off is a good-enough regime for most species, but if you are hoping to breed them you will have to vary the cycle throughout the year to bring them into condition.

Humidity

Humidity is a result of the amount of moisture in an enclosure versus the amount of ventilation. Enclosures that are sprayed often and have little ventilation will become humid, whereas those that are rarely sprayed and have plenty of ventilation will be dry. Bearded dragons are easy to cater for in this respect; they come from dry, arid places and these conditions are easy to meet in a vivarium. They do not need to be sprayed as a matter of course, and water bowls should be small to prevent too much evaporation.

Having said that, bearded dragons sometimes have problems when shedding their skin, especially on the tips of their tails and on their

Left: *This bearded dragon is shedding its skin. Some individuals seem to shed more easily if their cage is sprayed, whereas others seem to manage without the extra humidity. You will soon find a regime that suits your lizards.*

CREATING A DAMP RETREAT

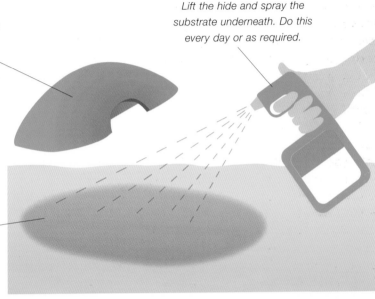

Species that have trouble shedding benefit from a little localised humidity and often seek out suitable places. Use a hide with a small cut-out section to create an area of high humidity.

Lift the hide and spray the substrate underneath. Do this every day or as required.

When the hide is replaced, water vapour will be trapped inside it, raising the humidity.

toes. Dry skin can constrict blood flow and it is not uncommon for the tips of the tails and toes to shrivel and fall off. This is obviously not ideal. If you have a bearded dragon that regularly has a problem shedding its skin from these extremities, you can spray the cage lightly when it is coming up to shed. Another technique is to use an artificial hide, such as a modified flower-pot, and spray the sand underneath every day or two to create a localised area of high humidity that the lizard can use if it feels the need.

Nevertheless, shedding problems are unusual in bearded dragons. If they occur it might be a good idea to check other factors. Is the correct substrate present? Is there somewhere rough, such as a rock, on which the lizard can rub itself to free dead pieces of skin? Shedding problems can also be caused by lizards that are weakened by diseases or parasites, or even nutritional problems, although this is less likely.

Species of dragon lizards from more humid environments, including rainforests, have completely different requirements. They should be sprayed daily, although the enclosure must still be adequately ventilated. A substrate that absorbs moisture and then releases it over a period of hours also helps. Additional notes are given in the appropriate species' profiles.

Housing dragon lizards

In this section we look at accommodation suitable for bearded dragons, as they are the main subject of this book. Variations on these designs will also be suitable for other dragon lizards and some of these are also noted here. These notes are expanded in the species profiles (pages 108-201).

Free-range dragons

Some people keep their bearded dragon 'free-range'. In other words, they let them have the run of their house, or at least one room in the house. This is not recommended for reasons of hygiene and safety. The animals can become trapped under furniture, get burnt, chilled or electrocuted. Other pets can kill them or they can find their way out of the house and escape. Every bearded dragon should have an enclosure and, if you like to take it out of the enclosure from time to time, only do this under careful supervision and for a limited time. Bearded dragons are territorial and taking them out of

their territory and placing them in a strange one can be stressful.

Enclosure size

Buying a bearded dragon, or a related species, involves a commitment to house it adequately. A cute baby bearded dragon of 20-30cm will rapidly turn into a large, strong and active adult, measuring anything up to 50cm and weighing up to 500gm in the case of older males. An enclosure, also called a vivarium, measuring 120cm long by 60cm wide and 60cm high should be regarded as the absolute minimum for one to three adult bearded dragons. Dimensions of 200x60x60cm, or even 200x100x100cm would be better and essential if you intend to keep a small group of, say, four or five together for any length of time.

Enclosures for juvenile bearded dragons (or for smaller species of dragon lizards) can be scaled down accordingly. In fact, providing accommodation for a growing bearded dragon

PLANNING FOR GROWTH

When planning a vivarium for bearded dragons, bear in mind that they grow quickly and will need larger housing as they grow.

CHOOSING THE RIGHT SHAPE

Ground-dwelling species, such as bearded dragons, need a large floor area.

A taller enclosure suits arboreal lizards, such as water dragons.

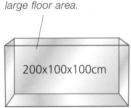

200x100x100cm

200x100x100cm

is a lot like potting on a houseplant: you start small and move them up as they grow. Small bearded dragons do better in small enclosures of about 60x30x30cm. In enclosures of this size

they are never far away from food, water and a heat source, and this avoids the possibility that shy individuals will sulk at one end. After a few months (depending on how quickly your dragon grows) it will be a subadult and you will need to move it on. Ideally, this should be to an intermediate-sized enclosure, say 100x50x50cm or thereabouts. By six to twelve months of age, the lizards should be approaching full size and can be housed permanently in an enclosure such as the one described above.

Positioning the enclosure

Most people will have limited choices when it comes to positioning their lizard enclosure. If you do have a choice, try to place it in a spot where the lizards will experience some light

Left: Bearded dragons can be kept together in small groups and will usually interact peacefully, once a pecking order is established.

POSITIONING THE ENCLOSURE

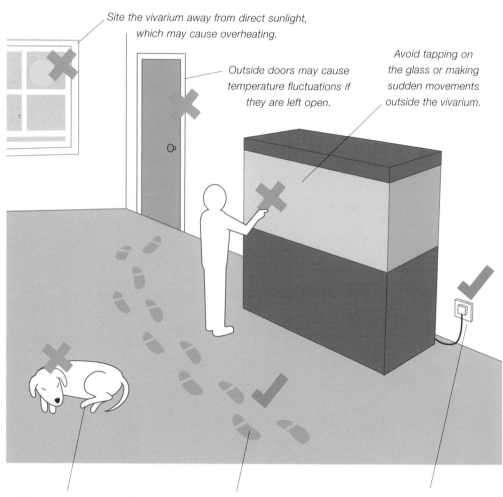

Site the vivarium away from direct sunlight, which may cause overheating.

Outside doors may cause temperature fluctuations if they are left open.

Avoid tapping on the glass or making sudden movements outside the vivarium.

Lizards regard dogs and cats as predators. They may become stressed if pets are constantly nearby.

A certain amount of normal human traffic past the vivarium will help the lizards get used to seeing people.

If possible, position the vivarium near a power point, for safety reasons.

human 'traffic' but that is not too noisy. Occasional passers-by will help the lizards get used to seeing people and make them less nervous when the time comes to service their enclosure. For obvious reasons, it is not a good idea to position the enclosure in a draught, nor should it be in a room that experiences major fluctuations in temperature every day. Avoid a position where rays from the sun can shine into the vivarium for more than a few minutes each day otherwise there is a danger that it may overheat. For safety reasons, the vivarium should be near a power point so that cables do not trail across the floor. If you have other pets, especially dogs and cats, which the lizards will see as predators, it is better to keep them away from the vivarium. Children sometimes like to bang on the glass fronts of vivariums and this should be discouraged.

Materials

There are a number of options when it comes to choosing a vivarium and all of them have advantages and disadvantages.

Above: Hatchling bearded dragons can be temporarily housed in open plastic boxes, which are freely available and cheap. Heating and lighting equipment can be clamped to the sides and the boxes are easy to wash and disinfect if necessary.

PLASTIC VIVARIUMS

Probably the best material for enclosures is moulded plastic with a sliding glass front. Enclosures of this type are relatively tough, light and can be washed out thoroughly. They do not contain nooks and crannies in which parasites can hide and it is relatively easy to fix lighting and heating to them. You can cut extra ventilation panels if required, and glue mesh over them. Apart from the front glass panels (which

A WOODEN VIVARIUM

Use plastic-faced wood that can be wiped down with a damp cloth.

The edges of sliding glass panels should be ground down to avoid accidents. Add a lock or catch if there are small children in the family.

The enclosure should be rigid and sturdy so that it does not warp, allowing draughts to come in (and lizards to get out).

Position some of the ventilation low down on the sides or back to allow carbon dioxide to escape.

The front should have a lip that is high enough to prevent substrate falling out.

you can replace easily if they get broken) they are almost indestructible when used as they are intended.

Depending on the design it is sometimes possible to stack enclosures or, failing this, to slot them into a purpose-built rack. When stacking them, it is important to make sure that ventilation panels are not obstructed. If they are on display in a living room you can build them into a cabinet, making an attractive piece of display furniture. However, enclosures of this type are expensive, and few people will want to buy the several sizes required for bearded dragons at all stages of their life. A compromise is to use a large moulded vivarium for adult

dragons, but to house the juveniles and sub-adults in less expensive enclosures.

WOODEN VIVARIUMS

A popular compromise is an enclosure made of plastic-faced chipboard or MDF, fitted with a sliding glass front. It has many of the advantages of a moulded plastic enclosure – it is fairly lightweight, it is possible to stack enclosures and equipment, and furnishings are easy to attach – but is harder to wash thoroughly or to disinfect. Nor will it probably last as long, as any dampness will cause the wood to swell and the plastic covering to lift.

Some lizard-keepers make their own wooden

enclosures tailored to specific requirements – to fit into an alcove, for instance – but if you decide to take this route, give careful thought to the design. The front should have a 10-15cm lip to prevent substrate from falling out each time you slide back the glass front and to prevent sand and gravel entering and clogging up the runners. It is a good idea to seal all the internal corners with a silicon aquarium sealer to prevent mites and other parasites from hiding in them and to enable more thorough cleaning. Ventilation panels should be fitted to the sides and back,

Above: *Forest dragons require taller vivariums, such as this commercially produced glass cube with front-opening doors. There are many suitable designs; some keepers prefer to make their own.*

and positioned low down. Top ventilation alone is unsatisfactory, as noxious gases – especially carbon dioxide – are heavier than air and will accumulate in the bottom few centimetres of the enclosure, right where the lizards are living.

GLASS VIVARIUMS

Glass vivariums are another alternative, but only the small sizes are light enough to be carried. Large ones are fine, provided they are intended to be permanent fixtures. Very large sizes are frighteningly heavy, so they must be well-supported on a sturdy table or stand and are best restricted to ground floors. As far as the design goes, this is largely down to personal taste, as long as you consider the species to be kept. Bearded dragons require as much floor space as possible, whereas arboreal dragon lizards benefit from tall enclosures. Once again, you need to make sure that there is plenty of ventilation low down in the sides, back or below the sliding glass doors.

A glass aquarium with added ventilation can be pressed into use and, if it is tall enough, you may find that there is no need to keep a lid on it as none of the ground-dwelling dragon lizards is able to climb glass (although heat will escape). Glass reptile vivariums with sliding doors are available, though quite expensive, and these are ideal for keeping one or a small group of juvenile bearded dragons. You can use them for other species in your collection once the dragons have outgrown them.

SETTING UP A BEARDED DRAGON ENCLOSURE

There are two schools of thought when it comes to setting up reptile enclosures. Some keepers prefer to keep things clean and clinical, whereas others make the enclosure recreate the natural habitat of the species concerned.

1. First gather together all the equipment you will need. There are many options and part of the enjoyment is in choosing items that will enhance the appearance of the vivarium as well as providing a suitable environment for the lizard.

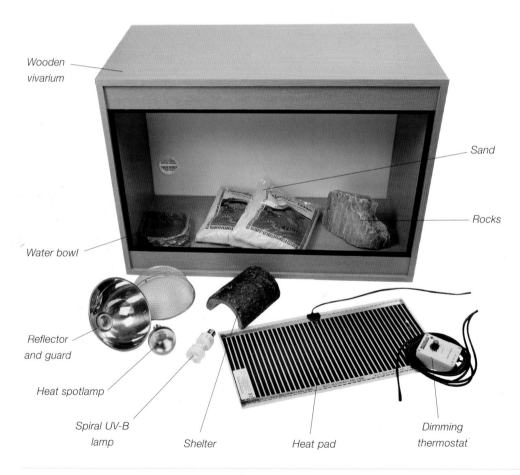

Wooden vivarium

Sand

Rocks

Water bowl

Reflector and guard

Heat spotlamp

Spiral UV-B lamp

Shelter

Heat pad

Dimming thermostat

2. *Place the vivarium on a level, solid surface. You may need to place a thin sheet of polystyrene underneath to prevent the vivarium wobbling. Slide a heat pad under one end and push it completely under the vivarium. Allow the connector block to protrude out the side or back.*

3. *Attach the thermostat to the outside of the vivarium, in a position where you can easily check and adjust it. A small heat pad gives off only a gentle heat and may not need controlling with a thermostat, but the basking lamp will usually require a thermostat, ideally a dimmer one, as here.*

If the base is very thick, you may need to attach the heat pad to the back panel, where the material will be thinner. However, this is a slightly less satisfactory method of providing heat.

By placing the pad at one end of the vivarium, the lizards will be able to move away from it in the unlikely event that they become too warm.

Make a small hole in the side or back of the vivarium and place the sensor about half way along the inside back wall, about 5cm up from the base.

The aim is to set the background temperature to the required level. The temperature beneath the basking lamp will be considerably higher in the day, when it is on.

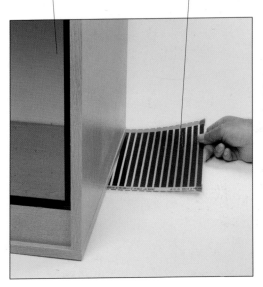

SUBSTRATE

Bearded dragons are fairly easy to cater for in this respect, because a naturalistic set-up for them should be easy to maintain and keep clean anyway. They live in deserts and semi-desert habitats, so a sand or gravel substrate is suitable, sand being the best choice for practical reasons. Use the sand sold specifically for reptiles, as it will be free from impurities and chemicals that are often found in builders' sand, for instance. 'Play sand' can be used safely.

The gut of very young bearded dragons can sometimes become impacted with sand that they take in accidentally with their food, in which case paper towels or newspaper, although not as pleasing to look at, are a better choice. By the time the dragons reach about 20cm in total length (10cm SVL) they can be moved to a sandy substrate, although they will not come to any harm if left on newspaper.

Cleaning enclosures with sand substrate is relatively easy, as faeces can be lifted out with a spoon or scoop. Keep one specifically for this purpose – do not 'borrow' one from the kitchen. After a few sessions of 'spot-cleaning', as it is called, you will need to top up the sand. Sooner or later, it will become dirty and unattractive and a complete change will be necessary.

Bark chippings are not recommended for bearded dragons because they often contain sharp splinters that become lodged in the animals' throats or damage their eyes. In addition, bark chippings create copious amounts of dark brown dust when they have been in an enclosure for a while. However, bark chippings are suitable for some other dragon lizards, especially arboreal forest dragons that rarely come down to ground level. Cedar and pine shavings, which give off noxious fumes when damp, should be avoided.

ROCKS

Bearded dragons also need rocks and stumps to perch and bask on. By making their enclosure varied you will give the lizards plenty of places to hide, bask or display, as the mood takes them. These are important aspects of their natural behaviour and they will become stressed if they are not given these opportunities in captivity. It will also make a more interesting display. Heating and lighting are discussed on pages 45-54, but from the point of view of vivarium layout, you should give the lizards opportunities to warm up and cool down, to bask in full light or to rest in the shade. Natural rocks retain heat better than artificial ones and, again, basking on a warm rock after the heater or light has gone off in the evening is a natural way of extending the animals' activity because it is what they do in the wild. Dragons' claws grow constantly and need contact with rough surfaces to wear them down.

If you use natural rocks, make sure you do not take them from places that are protected, such as national parks and certain parts of the coast. To be on the safe side, use only rocks from your garden or buy them from pet stores or garden

INSTALLING THE LIGHTING AND HEATING

Choose from the range of light and heating options shown here. See pages 50-53 for more details.

Ceramic heater
For heat but no visible light

Mercury vapour lamp
For heat, light and UV-B combined

Linear UV-B tube or spiral
For visible light and UV-B

Heat spotlamp
For heat and light

Infra-red lamp
For heat and red light

Checking the temperature

Once the heat pad and lamp are working, check the temperature in different parts of the vivarium – under the basking lamp, over the heat pad and at the cool end. Do this every hour or so until it has settled down. Consult the information relating to the species you are planning to keep and satisfy yourself that the temperature range is suitable before going any further. You can do quite a lot of fine-tuning, such as changing the heat pad for one of a different rating, changing the heat lamp, or raising or lowering the basking platform.

Spiral UV-B lamp

Heat spotlamp and reflector

4. *Position the UV-B lamp in such a way that when the lizard sits under the heat lamp it will also be basking in the light. Refer to pages 50-53 for information on the type and size of lamp needed because it varies with the species, and its distance from the basking area.*

5. *Install the heat lamp and reflector inside the vivarium at one end of the roof to provide a thermal gradient. Employ a qualified electrician if you are not confident of doing this yourself. It is a good idea to fit a grille over the reflector to prevent burns to the lizard and to anyone servicing the vivarium.*

centres. Rocks on which the lizards have been basking should be washed at the same time as the rest of the enclosure.

If you use rocks to decorate the enclosure you must ensure that they are safely arranged. A stack of flat rocks is better than a pile of irregular ones because it is not likely to collapse onto the lizards. Removing a flat basking rock to give it a good clean and perhaps disinfect

it is much easier than trying to dismantle a complicated 'rockery'. All this is common sense, but it is easy to get carried away when trying to make a vivarium look as attractive as possible. Remember, although they need a range of perches and places to bask and hide, bearded dragons are not known for their artistic appreciation; any efforts you make in this direction are solely to please the onlooker.

ADDING SAND AND ROCKS

6. *Before spreading sand over the base of the vivarium, place one or two heavy, flat rocks on the floor. This will prevent the lizards from undermining the rocks if they choose to dig.*

7. *Run the sand into the vivarium to a depth of at least 2-3cm.*

8. *With the first layer of rocks solidly positioned on the base of the vivarium, build up a rock-pile underneath the basking lights.*

Suitable rocks and shelters

You can use a wide variety of rocks and artificial hides to create a landscape within the enclosure. Research the natural habitat for ideas.

Place this part of this synthetic cave inside the enclosure, against the front glass.

Right: Take care with rounded rocks; they could fall and injure the lizards. Flat rocks are preferable.

Fit the cover to the outside glass and remove to reveal the lizard inside.

Right: Artificial hides are available in a variety of shapes, sizes and materials and will be used by lizards that require shelter from the heat or from other members of their group.

This shape is ideal for creating a damp retreat as shown on page 55.

ADDING THE WATER BOWL AND HIDE

9. When you are happy with the look of the rock pile and have checked that it is stable, place a water bowl at the end furthest away from the heating. Add a hide, which can be a piece of curved bark, an artificial structure or a rock cave.

10. Once you are satisfied that the temperature and lighting equipment is working properly, add the lizard!

Below: Once the heat lamp has warmed up, the bearded dragon will soon seek out a suitable basking area.

THE FINISHED ENCLOSURE

*Here is the finished vivarium, complete with everything the lizard needs.
This size (100x75x45cm) is suitable for one to three juvenile bearded
dragons, or other lizards of similar size. Use a similar layout regardless
of the size of the vivarium.*

*Heat spotlamp with
reflector and mesh
guard.*

Ventilation at a low level is ideal.

UV-B spiral lamp

*A water bowl is essential and this is
best positioned away from the heat
source. Change the water and rinse
out the bowl every day.*

*The animals will also
appreciate a shelter or two
that allows them to get away
from the heat and light.*

*This pile of rocks is
ideally positioned under
the heater at one end of
the enclosure.*

PLANTS FOR BEARDED DRAGONS

Adding plants to a naturalistic setup is an appealing idea and when it is done well it will enhance the look of the vivarium. However, there is one obvious drawback when it comes to planting out bearded dragons' vivariums: they eat plants. The best solution is to use tough plants, such as Mother-in-law's Tongue (*Sansevieria trifasciata*) or, even better, the Bird's Nest Sansevieria (*S. trifasciata hahnii*), which has shorter and wider leaves. Either of these can withstand the tramplings of large bearded dragons and are too fibrous for them to eat. Even so, they will not survive indefinitely in the hot, dry environment of a bearded dragon's enclosure and it is better to leave them in their pots and rotate them between the enclosure and a bright windowsill or conservatory.

Other possibilities include some palms and strong-growing succulents, perhaps some of the more vigorous aloe and agave species, but be prepared to remove them if they get nibbled or damaged. Cactus are not recommended.

The dab lizards (*Uromastyx*) are also herbivores and will eat almost any plant material, including twigs and bark, so it is unlikely that even *Sansevieria* will survive long in their enclosure.

Enclosures for other dragon lizards

Much of what has been said above also applies to other species of dragon lizards. However, you should give some consideration to these animals' normal habitat. For example, climbing species will require tall vivariums with plenty of

Above: *Tough succulent plants, such as Bird's Nest Sansevieria, are suitable for bearded dragon enclosures.*

PLASTIC PLANTS *Plastic plants are decorative, durable and easy to wash.*

upright branches, whereas ground-dwellers, in common with bearded dragons, require a large surface area. Many species are not as showy and confident as bearded dragons, especially if they are not captive-bred, and they should be given plenty of places to hide. Forcing them out into the open will not help them adapt to captivity.

SUBSTRATE

The best substrate for forest dragon enclosures is orchid bark, or a mixture of roughly equal parts by volume of orchid bark and sand. Coconut fibre, or coir, is another possibility but, like peat, this substance is difficult to wet once it has dried out. It is usually available in the form of a brick of compressed fibre, which you soak overnight in a bucket of water. This causes it to expand in size almost magically. If you use this, it works better if you make sure the substrate never dries out completely. Coir could also be mixed with sand or orchid bark.

2. This model includes a lid, or hood, with fittings for two compact fluorescent lamps. At least one of these should provide light in the ultraviolet B part of the spectrum. The other can be a plain white light, which gives a warmer appearance. Lighting is most easily controlled by a time-switch and the day length can be varied throughout the year, giving the lizards a natural seasonal change.

1. With smaller types of vivarium, provided they have a mesh top, place the heat-lamp on the lid, out of the reach of the inhabitants. However, if the vivarium is taller, there may be room for the heat-lamp inside, as long as it is shielded to prevent the lizards from coming into contact with it.

PLANTS FOR DRAGON LIZARDS

Dragon lizards from humid tropical regions give you more scope in this area as they do not eat plants, and the warm, moist conditions suit a number of species usually sold as houseplants. These include various species of *Philodendron, Monstera,* figs, especially the weeping fig *Ficus benjamina*, and many others. These can be bought cheaply at garden centres and supermarkets. The plants should be large and robust, otherwise the lizards will destroy them, or their food, such as crickets and locusts, will eat them. Again, the plants will do better if they are left in their pots rather than planted directly into the substrate of the enclosure so that they can be removed occasionally.

Some epiphytes, such as stag's horn ferns *(Platycerium* species*)* can be attached to pieces of bark or tree-fern root and hung on the side or back of the vivarium. If you have a subsidiary interest in exotic plants – and many reptile keepers do – you will have plenty of opportunities to try interesting plants in the enclosures. Do not use plant foods to spray the foliage of plants inside lizard enclosures and it should be obvious that insecticides and pesticides must not be used on them either.

SUITABLE TYPES OF WOOD

Pieces of wood and bark give the lizards something to climb on and add interest to the enclosure. Wash them occasionally and replace them if they become very soiled or if there are infections or parasites in the colony.

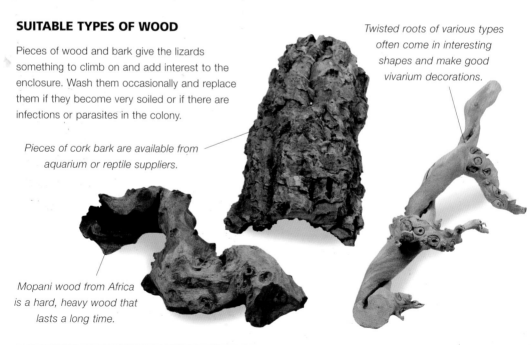

Twisted roots of various types often come in interesting shapes and make good vivarium decorations.

Pieces of cork bark are available from aquarium or reptile suppliers.

Mopani wood from Africa is a hard, heavy wood that lasts a long time.

Bark chippings should be of a good-quality 'orchid bark' grade, and free from dust or splinters. If this is hard to obtain, choose coir or leaf-litter.

3. *Add the substrate – here we are using orchid bark – to a suitable depth.*

4. *Place a water bowl and branch into the vivarium. If the cage is large, several pieces of branch would be more appropriate. If the vivarium is to house water dragons, provide a considerably bigger water bowl, as much as half the floor area. Large adults, would need a container deep enough for them soak in.*

THE FINISHED ENCLOSURE

Add some foliage, which can be natural or artificial, to give the forest dragon an opportunity to hide. By spraying the leaves you enable the lizard to lick droplets of water, as sometimes they are reluctant to use a water bowl. For shy lizards, add enough foliage so that they can remain completely hidden if this is what they prefer. They will gradually become more confident, provided they know they can return to the safety of their hideaway.

Right: Small commercially available enclosures are suitable for hatchling and small juvenile forest dragons. Larger enclosures will be required as the lizard grows and can be quite expensive.

This simple design has all the main elements to make a forest dragon feel at home.

Left: A forest-type set-up such as this, with artificial plants, some branches and perhaps a background image, can be an interesting addition to a living room, but make sure that the lizards have places to hide.

Cleaning the enclosure

The interval between thorough cleans will depend on the size of the vivarium, how many animals are housed in it, and how much spot-cleaning you have done in the meantime. This is the time to wipe down the inside of the enclosure completely and to scrub any other 'furniture' that may have become soiled, using a dilute solution of bleach disinfectant if you wish. Newspaper, of course, is even more easily and cheaply changed. It is often possible to clean one portion of the vivarium at a time, allowing the lizards to move to the other end while you do so. Tame lizards can be taken out of the vivarium while it is cleaned and held by another member of the family or simply placed in a large container. If you have used strong-smelling disinfectant or cleaner (which is rarely necessary) then it is a good idea to keep the lizard(s) out of the vivarium until the smell has dissipated completely.

Feeding dragon lizards

Wild bearded dragons eat insects, small vertebrates (especially smaller lizards) and plant material. Youngsters eat more insects than plants but, as they grow, the availability of insect food is not enough to satisfy their appetites. As a result, their diet gradually includes more plant material, which can account for 80% of their intake, by volume. In captivity, bearded dragons would eat nothing but insects given the chance, and some keepers allow them to do this. However, a more natural diet includes a variety of foodstuffs, together with supplements. Generally speaking, plants have less protein than insects but more fibre and a better range of vitamins and minerals. However, plants are more difficult to digest and plant-eating animals need to eat more, so you should offer them plenty. If they eat it all, offer them more and increase the amount given in the future.

Insect food

Live foods for lizards are widely sold by specialist dealers and general pet shops. The mainstay is crickets, which are available in various sizes and several different species; locusts; mealworms (the larvae of a beetle, *Tenebrio molitor*); giant

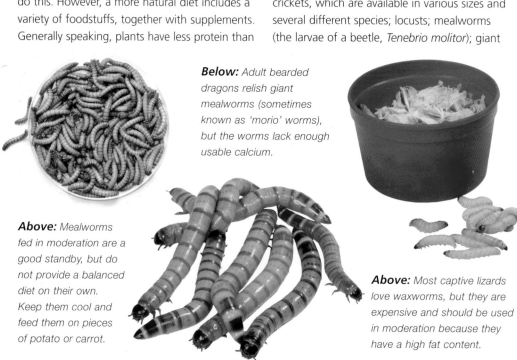

Below: *Adult bearded dragons relish giant mealworms (sometimes known as 'morio' worms), but the worms lack enough usable calcium.*

Above: *Mealworms fed in moderation are a good standby, but do not provide a balanced diet on their own. Keep them cool and feed them on pieces of potato or carrot.*

Above: *Most captive lizards love waxworms, but they are expensive and should be used in moderation because they have a high fat content.*

mealworms (the larvae of a related beetle, *Zophobas morio*); and waxworms (the larva of a moth, *Galleria mellonella*). Other feeder insects might occasionally be sold. All these are suitable for bearded dragons. Crickets are the most popular because they are lively and give the lizards something to chase, which is a good thing, and because they are easy to dust with vitamins. Locusts are larger than crickets and more suitable for large bearded dragons.

Above: *An Inland Bearded Dragon* (Pogona vitticeps) *taking a mealworm from its owner's fingers. These lizards are very responsive, especially when a favourite food item is on offer!*

Mealworms, including giant mealworms, are not as nutritious as they lack calcium in an easily digestible form. Nevertheless, newly moulted mealworms, which are white in colour, are better than the yellow ones with hardened skins.

Waxworms are high in fat and should not be used exclusively, even though the lizards seem to like them. They can be pressed into use if you have a lizard that has lost its appetite, but beware of conditioning lizards to expect waxworms all the time.

CATCHING INVERTEBRATES

You can add to the above selection by catching invertebrates from a 'safe' habitat, such as your garden, where they will not have come into contact with chemicals. Grasshoppers, beetles and spiders can be caught by hand and livelier species can be caught in a sweep net. However, the mass of small flying insects that end up in a sweep net are of little use to bearded dragons (but you might be able to use them for other dragon lizards or other reptiles and amphibians if you have any).

STORING AND CONDITIONING INVERTEBRATE FOODS

Wild food is varied and nourishing and should contain all the minerals and vitamins your lizards need. However, crickets, locusts and mealworms will be supplied in a plastic box with a small amount of bran. The bran gives the insects something to chew on but is hardly nutritious. If you feed these insects to the lizards as soon as you buy them, the lizards, in turn, will not be obtaining much in the way of nourishment either. For this reason, you should place the insects in a suitable container, such as a ventilated plastic box or cage, and feed

> ### Rodents as food
>
> *Adult bearded dragons will also eat small rodents, which can be stored frozen and thawed out as necessary. However, these are not an essential part of their diet and should be used sparingly.*

them with vegetables before giving them to the lizards. Sliced carrots are a good food for crickets and mealworms, but almost any vegetable that is not too soft will be better than bran alone. You can also give them rabbit pellets or other dried pet food. Locusts prefer leafy vegetables or grass.

A good method is to keep a stock of insects as described, but to place enough for one feed into a small box with high-protein foods such as bee pollen (obtainable from health food

Below: Crickets will be more nourishing if they have been 'gut-loaded' with a food supplement or a variety of vegetables, before being given to the lizards. Bee pollen and insect gel are just two possible ways of increasing their value.

Left: *Keep crickets in a container with food and water. Here, the tubes are used to transfer crickets to the lizards.*

suppliers) the night before you give them to the lizards. The insects will eat this and it will still be in their gut when the lizards feed on them. Alternatively, there are several foodstuffs marketed specifically for this purpose, described as 'gut-loading'.

CRICKETS

Crickets are usually sold in plastic boxes or tubs containing a variable number depending on their size. Only the adults have wings (although none of them fly) and only the males 'sing'. Adult females can be recognised by the presence of a long egg-tube, or ovipositor. In the UK there are at least three species of crickets sold for reptile food. Some pet shops stock all three, others only stock one.

The common house cricket *(Acheta domestica)* is the smallest species and can become a pest in the home if it escapes. However, it is the most prolific species and boxes of these will probably contain more crickets than boxes of the other species. This species is sometimes sold under the name of the banded brown cricket.

The Mediterranean field cricket *(Gryllus bimaculatus)* is a large black species that can be quite noisy, although it is unlikely to survive or breed if it escapes in the home. The so-called quiet cricket *(Gryllus assimilis)* is not quite as noisy as either of the other two species, although it is not completely silent. All of these crickets are equally good as food, provided they are well fed beforehand and dusted with supplement powder immediately before being given to the lizards.

LOCUSTS

Two species of locust are bred for the pet trade: the migratory locust *(Locusta migratoria)* and the desert locust *(Schistocerca gregaria)*. Neither will

Right: *Reptile dealers sell crickets of various sizes in plastic containers.*

Below: *Offer the locusts soon after buying them. Otherwise, store them in a large, warm, well-ventilated cage and feed them with fresh grass.*

Crickets and locusts

As a matter of interest, crickets sing (the scientific term is stridulate) by rubbing their wing cases together, whereas locusts stridulate by rubbing their back legs together, as do grasshoppers. Locusts are simply grasshoppers that swarm.

Vegetable food

Bearded dragons in the wild, especially when they are adult, eat leaves and flowers. In captivity, leafy vegetables, such as cress, dandelion leaves, groundsel, clover and alfalfa, are the most natural foods. Chopped or grated carrots and almost any vegetables sold for human consumption are also suitable in small quantities. Soft fruits, such as bananas, are not recommended for frequent use as often they do

become a pest if it escapes and males of both species sing or 'chirp'. Either species is equally suitable as a food for bearded dragons, although they are more expensive than crickets. Subadult locusts are usually known as 'hoppers' and can be fed on grass or green vegetables before being fed to the lizards.

not contain enough fibre.

Before giving them to the lizards, wash the leaves and skins of vegetables in case they have

Below: An Inland Bearded Dragon feeding from a bowl of mixed chopped salad. The bowl needs to be emptied and replenished on a daily basis.

Below: Vitamin and mineral supplements of various makes are available. Although their exact formulations may vary slightly, any of the well-known brands will give good results. Some keepers like to buy two or more different makes and alternate them.

Above: One way of dusting live foods with vitamin and mineral supplements is to place them in a plastic freezer bag with the powder and shake them up before feeding them to the lizards.

chemicals on them. You will often find that given a choice, bearded dragons and some other species will fill up on insects and then refuse the vegetable food. The best way to encourage them to eat it is to withhold their insect meal and just offer a tray of mixed leaves and vegetables once every three or four days, for instance. Larger bearded dragons tend to be more willing to take vegetable material than youngsters and can be offered it every day if they will take it.

Food supplements

Lizards in the wild eat a wide variety of food that provides them with all the ingredients they need to stay healthy. However, cultured foods, such as crickets, are always lacking in essential vitamins and minerals and, on their own, do not constitute a balanced diet. Although giving the animals a variety of foods will help, you will also need to supplement their diet with a vitamin and mineral mixture. There are many of these on the market, aimed specifically at reptiles, and they all contain a wide spectrum of trace elements, vitamins and minerals. Lightly dust every insect and plant meal with one of these products at every feed. Because they vary slightly in their formulae, it can be a good idea to buy two or three makes and alternate them.

Left: All lizards, even desert-dwellers such as bearded dragons, must have clean, drinking water available at all times. Replace it every day to avoid the risk of contamination and cross infection.

CALCIUM

Even so, these supplements rarely contain enough calcium, especially for growing lizards, which need calcium to form their skeletons, or for breeding females, which need it produce their eggs. For this reason, you should provide extra calcium in the form of a supplement, sprinkled over the animals' food. This is available from a specialist reptile dealer or you can make your own using cuttlefish bone. Fast-growing juveniles and breeding females need this every other day (in addition to the multi-vitamin and mineral supplement). Fully grown, non-breeding lizards need only one or two helpings each week. Some dragons eat 'raw' calcium if you leave a small dish of it in their cage.

As discussed in *Creating the right environment* (page 50) calcium is of no use to a lizard unless it also has a source of Vitamin D$_3$, which helps it to absorb the calcium into its body in a form that it can use. Some dietary supplements contain Vitamin D$_3$, but by far the best, and most natural, source of Vitamin D$_3$ is via ultraviolet light, especially UV-B. Lack of Vitamin D$_3$ or calcium will cause dietary problems, the first signs of which are lethargy and spasms. Weak and deformed skeletons will follow later and the lizard will eventually die if the condition is not corrected. See also *Health care* (pages 88-90).

Water

Bearded dragons should have access to clean drinking water at all times. Although they come from dry places and obtain much of their fluid intake from their food, the safest course is to make sure they can drink whenever they want to. Supply water in a shallow pan, rather than

Right: *Large water bowls allow lizards to soak. This is essential for certain forest and water dragons, but most species appreciate it, especially in the period before they shed their skins.*

Left: *Water bowls are available in many shapes and sizes. Any shallow dish can be pressed into service as long as it can be washed thoroughly.*

a small bowl, as the animals sometimes like to climb in completely and lower their heads to drink. This will also give them an opportunity to soak if they are about to shed their skin. It also means that they easily foul their water, so you must

Right: *Cuttlefish bone, as given to cage birds, can also add natural calcium to the diet of lizards. Shave small flakes from the bone and sprinkle them over food.*

remove the pan, wash it thoroughly and replace it with clean water every day. There is no need to sterilise or disinfect the pan unless there are signs of disease.

Some hatchling bearded dragons seem unable to recognise standing water but will lick drops from the sides of their cage, so a slight misting every morning will be appreciated. Similarly, you should rinse their plant food with fresh water and give it to the animals while it is

83

still wet. This also helps the vitamin and mineral powders to stick to the food better.

A feeding routine

It is a good idea to keep to a fixed feeding regime. Once the basking lights come on in the morning the lizards will spend the first 10 to 20 minutes warming up. Then they start looking for food and this is the time to feed them. Insects dusted with supplements will try to clean themselves, so the quicker the lizards eat them the better. If you put in the crickets before the lizards have warmed up properly, there will be a delay. Similarly, if you put too many crickets into the cage some will survive into the next day, by which time they will have completely cleaned off the supplements, and any food in their gut will have worked its way out of their system. For the same reason, if spraying the cage is part of your routine, do it first thing, before you put in the insects, otherwise the water will simply wash the supplements off the insects.

Below: An Inland Bearded Dragon eats dandelion leaves. As long as they have not been sprayed with chemicals, garden weeds are a useful source of free food. Bearded dragons and dab lizards especially appreciate dandelion flowers.

A typical care regime

1. In the morning: the light comes on, either manually or by means of a time switch.

2. Spray the cage at this time if necessary.

3. Wash and replenish the water dish.

4. About 20-30 minutes later, supply food. If this consists of insects, dust them with a good-quality vitamin and mineral powder and/or calcium. Put in enough to be eaten in about 10 minutes, so they get the benefit of the supplements before they are cleaned off.

If the food for the day is vegetable material, wash and chop it if necessary, dust it with supplement and place it on a tray positioned away from the basking spot so that it stays fresh for longer.

5. During the day the lizards bask.

6. At the end of the day: remove uneaten vegetable food, which will have wilted.

7. In the evening: the light goes off, either manually or by means of a time switch.

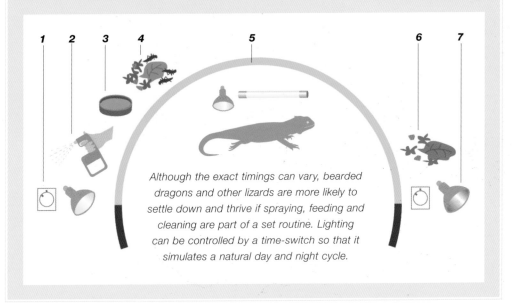

Although the exact timings can vary, bearded dragons and other lizards are more likely to settle down and thrive if spraying, feeding and cleaning are part of a set routine. Lighting can be controlled by a time-switch so that it simulates a natural day and night cycle.

Health care

The first thing that needs to be said here is that if you suspect your bearded dragon or other dragon lizard has a disease, the most sensible course of action is to get it to a veterinarian as soon as possible. Veterinarians have the necessary experience, equipment and access to drugs to deal with serious diseases. Treating an animal yourself is not recommended for anything other than the most straightforward problems and any advice offered here is given with that understanding.

Having said that, the main causes of health problems in bearded dragons are an incorrect environment or an inadequate diet. If you have had your lizards for several weeks or months, and have not introduced any new lizards to the colony, then it is highly unlikely that they will have contracted a disease. If you do introduce new animals, carry out the quarantine procedure described on page 35 and, again, any problems are unlikely to be due to contagious diseases.

What to look out for

Your main weapon in the quest for speedy diagnosis of health problems, and their treatment, is observation. Once you get to know your animals it should be relatively easy to spot abnormal behaviour that might be due to health problems and deal with these before they become serious. A healthy bearded dragon should be active, alert and hungry. Its eyes

should be bright and it should have plenty of flesh on its bones, especially in the region at the base of its tail and on its thighs. The toes should be complete and not swollen. The faeces should be firm and the area around the vent should be clean. The bearded dragon should not have any trouble in shedding its skin periodically. If, on the other hand, your pet is lethargic, stops basking and eating, has dull and sunken eyes, and the area around its vent is smeared with loose faeces and it begins to lose weight, problems may be developing. If you deal with these as soon as they appear they often clear up on their own.

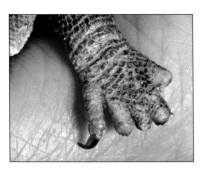

Above: *This dab lizard has lost digits because the conditions were too dry when it was shedding its skin. They have healed, but the claws will not grow back.*

Shedding problems

Lizards that are not in good health, or whose environment is too dry, sometimes have problems shedding their skin. This can result in dead skin remaining on their toes and the tip of their tail. If the problem is not corrected, the dead skin will contract, stopping the blood supply to the areas concerned, eventually leading to dead tissue. If you notice a lizard with pieces of dead skin on its toes, soak it in a shallow bowl, or put it in a plastic box with a handful of moist sphagnum moss for about half an hour, and then gently pull the dead skin off piece by piece. It might be necessary to do this over two or three sessions.

Prevention is better than cure! If you notice lizards that do not shed their skin easily, lightly spraying the substrate under a favoured hiding place, such as a rock, log or artificial hide box, often helps. Remember that even those species that come from a desert environment often dig burrows that lead down to a level where the soil retains a small amount of moisture. Although it is not usually possible to duplicate these conditions in captivity, a small area of slightly damp substrate will serve the same purpose.

Where the skin has come away the area is brighter.

The skin on the flanks and hind legs will come away shortly.

Above: This Inland Bearded Dragon is shedding its skin. This pattern of shedding is perfectly normal and is an indication of a healthy lizard.

Health check list

Here are the checks to make as soon as you suspect things are not as they should be:

- **The temperature immediately under the heater.** There should be a hot-spot of between 40°C and 45°C within 30 minutes of the heater being switched on in the morning.

- **The background temperature at night.** This should be between 20°C and 30°C over most of the enclosure and there should be cooler places where the lizards can get away from the heat if they want to.

- **UV-B light.** Make sure there is an adequate source of UV-B: the UV-B emitting lamp should be within 20cm of the basking spot and should be of a suitable output (5-10%). It should be left on for the whole day. Make sure the lamp is not more than 12 months old.

- **Food and water.** Make sure the lizards are getting food and water. If one of a group of is sulking, it might be because more dominant members of the group are preventing it from feeding. The only cure is to remove the individual and put it in a cage on its own.

- **Food supplements.** Make sure the lizards are receiving enough vitamins and minerals, especially calcium, by dusting every feed with a high-quality powder formulated for lizards.

Calcium deficiency

If all these parameters are in order and the lizard is still behaving abnormally, the first thing to check is its calcium balance. Young dragons that do not receive enough calcium start to twitch and have fits of temporary paralysis, especially when handled. Even before this, they may suffer from constipation and a swollen belly, although this is not always easy to spot. These symptoms are the results of insufficient calcium to keep the muscles working properly. Muscle tone is needed to push food through the digestive system, as well as to operate the limbs. If the problem is not corrected quickly the lizard's skeleton will be affected, because the body takes calcium from the bones as it tries to keep the nervous system working. Limbs become deformed and the jaws become soft. When the animal tries to feed it is unable to crush its food.

In adult dragons, calcium deficiency results in weak and deformed bones. It is most common

Right: *This bearded dragon is showing the typical signs of severe metabolic bone disease. Its skeleton is deformed, its limbs and jaws are weak and soft, and its eyes are sunken and half closed. Once they reach this stage, bearded dragons are unlikely to recover.*

in breeding females because they require calcium to form their eggs and, if they cannot obtain it from their diet, they start to metabolise their own bones. Remember that the lizard must be able to use the calcium in its diet. To do this, it must have access to Vitamin D_3, which is most easily provided through UV-B basking lamps as described on page 50.

However, whether due to lack of calcium or lack of Vitamin D_3, the end result is the same: the lizard becomes calcium-deficient and immediate action is called for. Before doing anything else, replace the UV-B lamp with a new one with a higher output, or move it closer to the basking spot. It is hard to overdose on Vitamin D_3, so err on the side of too much rather than too little.

Make sure the lizard uses the basking place. The obvious way to do this is to direct plenty of heat onto it and encourage the lizard to bask. If it refuses to bask you can fix up another lamp

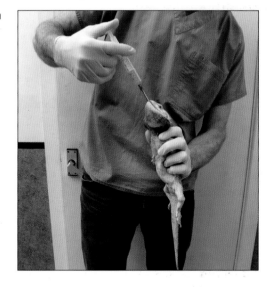

Above: *Tube feeding a bearded dragon. Sometimes called gavage feeding. Powdered nutritional support diets are now commercially available to provide nutritional support to bearded dragons that are not eating while they get better.*

just above the floor of the cage. Simply wire up a UV-B fluorescent tube temporarily (but safely) and suspend it just above the substrate. These measures are often enough to liven up the lizard and improve its appetite.

Now you need to make sure that the lizard's diet includes enough calcium by increasing the dose. Use a calcium supplement in addition to a multivitamin and mineral supplement. If things have become desperate, you can ask a veterinarian to force-feed a calcium solution or inject Vitamin D_3 to boost the dragon's metabolism. If you catch the problem in time, the dragon will sometimes recover fully and be back to normal within a few weeks. If, however, the skeleton has been weakened significantly, recovery will be much more unlikely as kidney damage, and other medical problems, may already have occurred. Even if the lizard does recover it may always have crooked limbs or a kinked tail and deformed jaws.

Internal parasites

Having dealt with the most common health problem affecting bearded dragons, we can turn our attention to a couple of medical issues that occasionally arise. The most important of these are caused by parasites.

COCCIDIOSIS

The most common of these problems is coccidiosis, which is caused by a protozoan parasite that lives in the lizard's gut. The outward signs are diarrhoea and, as a result, dehydration. A laboratory examination of the faeces will be necessary to confirm the presence of the coccidia. It is not necessarily life-threatening, but will eventually cause weight loss and lower the lizard's resistance to other diseases.

The parasite's life cycle involves the formation of cysts that are voided by the lizard in its faeces. If these are ingested by another lizard, or the same one, the cysts hatch and the infestation is perpetuated. Numbers can potentially build up to serious levels. It follows from this that the key to eliminating coccidiosis, or at least reducing its impact, is to break the life cycle by keeping the lizards scrupulously clean.

- Remove faeces as soon as you see them.
- Change the water in the dish every day or sooner if the lizard soils it.
- Remove trays of plant food if soiled.

This simple regime will prevent serious outbreaks of coccidiosis. To eliminate it entirely may require treating the lizards with drugs. Sulpha-based compounds are sometimes used, but they can have harmful side-effects and most veterinarians prefer more modern treatments, such as Toltrazuril (known by a number of trade names). Faecal samples should be submitted at regular intervals afterwards to make sure there is no residual infestation that might flare up again. Luckily, the drugs are relatively cheap to buy and appear to have no side-effects. If one lizard in a collection is affected, assume that the others will be too and treat them all.

PINWORMS

Pinworms are a kind of parasitic roundworm that live in the lizards' gut, feeding on the contents. They can often be seen in the faeces as very small, white worms with pointed heads. Small numbers can probably be ignored, but large infestations can cause weight loss and should be treated with a prescription-only drug.

COCCIDIOSIS LIFE CYCLE

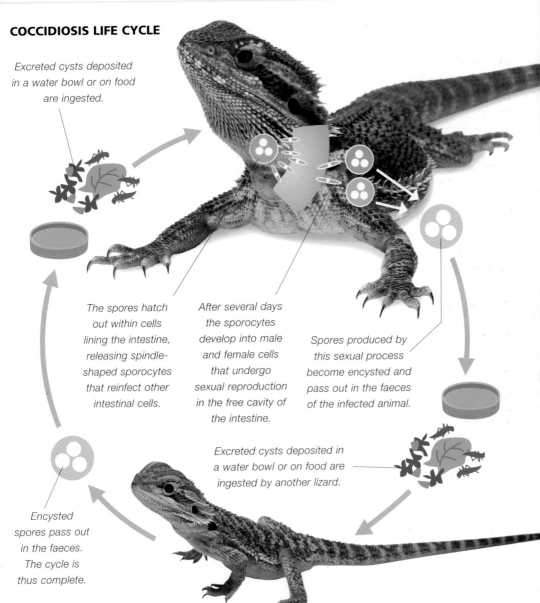

Excreted cysts deposited in a water bowl or on food are ingested.

The spores hatch out within cells lining the intestine, releasing spindle-shaped sporocytes that reinfect other intestinal cells.

After several days the sporocytes develop into male and female cells that undergo sexual reproduction in the free cavity of the intestine.

Spores produced by this sexual process become encysted and pass out in the faeces of the infected animal.

Excreted cysts deposited in a water bowl or on food are ingested by another lizard.

Encysted spores pass out in the faeces. The cycle is thus complete.

External parasites

Mites do not normally infest bearded dragons, but if you also have snakes in your collection the snake mite *Ophionyssus natricis* may move across to the lizards. The mites are unlikely to be a serious problem, but may linger in the lizards' enclosure and become a reservoir of re-infestation for the snakes. In any case, it is as well to eliminate them by keeping the vivarium clean, paying special attention to any nooks and crannies that the mite may hide in, and treating the animals with an ivermectin-based drug, obtained from a veterinarian and administered according to the instructions. Pesticide strips that used to be effective in their elimination are no longer available in many parts of the world for safety reasons.

Yellow fungus disease

In recent years, a new disease has been infecting bearded dragons. Although it is commonly called 'yellow fungus disease', it may be caused by more than one agent. However, the most common cause is a particular form of a fungus called *Nannizziopsis vriesii* and the correct name for the disease is 'necrotising mycotic dermatitis'. Symptoms start off with general lack of appetite and lethargy, followed by the development of yellow patches of skin. These patches increase in size and turn brown or black as the fungus digests the scales and underlying skin. Eventually they become extensive and the animal may die of secondary infections. As with all diseases, be sure to isolate infected animals, as the disease can be contagious. Also take precautions when

Right: *This bearded dragon has become infected with a fungus or bacteria that is eating away at its scales and flesh. Such infections can be difficult to diagnose and treat, and necessitate a visit to a veterinarian before they spread.*

Eight-month-old bearded dragon of normal weight and size.

An under weight eight-month-old bearded dragon.

Above: *The juvenile bearded dragon (right) has not grown as quickly as it should; compare it with the other lizard (left), which is the same age. There could be several reasons for its poor growth. If it has not been given enough food, it will recover and soon make up for lost time. On the other hand, it could have a calcium deficiency that has caused its jaws to become weak, thus preventing it from feeding properly.*

handling infected animals, as there is some evidence that the infection can affect humans.

Seek veterinary advice immediately if you notice sores or infected patches of skin on a lizard, as most treatments are only effective if they are given before the infection progresses too far. Certain drugs appear to be effective if used in the early stages and new forms of treatment are being researched. Meanwhile, this disease represents a serious threat to bearded dragons in captivity, making the advice regarding quarantine of new acquisitions especially relevant. Note, however, that this is by no means a widespread disease at the time of writing and, with sensible precautions when selecting new lizards, most keepers will never encounter it.

93

Breeding dragon lizards

Persuading your animals to breed is one of the most satisfying parts of keeping bearded dragons, or any other species for that matter. Firstly, it shows that you are looking after them properly and that you have provided all the necessary conditions for reproduction to take place. Secondly, you have the pleasure of following the complete life cycle, from mating, egg laying and incubating the eggs to seeing the young dragons hatching out and beginning a new generation. Thirdly, you may be able to selectively breed from especially colourful or vigorous specimens, thereby improving the strain and, finally, you can sell or exchange some of the youngsters to help fund your hobby.

Fortunately, although breeding any reptiles

can present certain challenges, bearded dragons are amongst the most straightforward species to breed if you follow a few simple rules. The whole process is divided into a number of stages.

Sex determination

Obviously, before you can hope to breed bearded dragons or related species, you must have at least one male and one female. Male bearded dragons do not have the secondary sex characteristics, such as crests, frills or horns, seen in some other species. In fact, they look very similar to the females, especially in the case of immature animals. Sex determination in juveniles is difficult but not impossible, but it becomes easier as they grow.

In common with all reptiles, male bearded dragons have paired copulatory organs, known as hemipenes. These are normally inverted (i.e. inside out) and rest in the base of the tail, with their openings just behind the cloaca, or vent. When the animals are mating, one or other of the hemipenes is pushed out of the vent (everted) so that copulation can occur. Once you know how to detect the presence of inverted hemipenes, sex determination becomes simple in older dragons, but can still be difficult in hatchlings and juveniles because differences are not great.

The easiest way to sex a lizard is to place it on a flat surface, with its head facing away

HIDDEN MALE SEX ORGANS

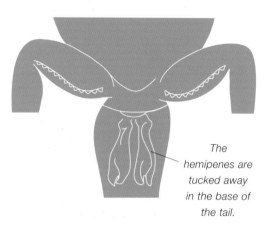

The hemipenes are tucked away in the base of the tail.

from you. Now grasp its tail about half way along and gently bend it upwards, at the same time raising the area of the vent off the ground. If the lizard is a male, two elongated bulges should be visible, running up the base of the tail with a groove between them. It has to be said that some people are better at this technique than others and that, as the lizard grows, the differences become more obvious. By the time they are about half-grown anyone should be able to tell the difference.

At this stage you may also be able to notice a difference in the shape of the tails, with those of males being parallel immediately behind the vent and then tapering quite sharply, whereas those of females taper more evenly.

As the animals approach maturity, the vent tends to be wider in males than it is in females. By this stage, males will have wider heads than females and their beards will usually be darker,

SEXING BEARDED DRAGONS

Male: *Note the shallow groove running down the base of the tail, outlining the inverted hemipenes.*

Female: *This Inland Bearded Dragon is a female. Note the more rounded cross-section of the tail.*

sometimes almost black. They also develop pre-anal pores just above the vent and femoral pores on the undersides of their thighs. Mature males tend to be more assertive than females and it is usually possible to tell them apart simply from watching the way in which they interact.

Breeding groups

For most people keeping bearded dragons as pets (i.e. not for commercial breeding) a pair of animals or one male and two females will be the most manageable way to keep and breed them. If they are reared together, the dominance hierarchy will develop naturally and courtship will ensue as they approach maturity. Although bearded dragons can potentially breed at about six months of age, a slower growth rate is better, so that breeding size is achieved at about 12 to 18 months of age. If you are in too much of a hurry, your lizards may breed more quickly but they will also burn out sooner.

Mating and gestation

In Europe and North America lizard breeding activity begins in the spring, so if you have bought your animals as juveniles in the summer of year one, they will start to breed in the spring of year three. You do not have to do anything to get them breeding, other than feed them well and make sure their environment is suitable, as outlined elsewhere. Pay particular attention to the calcium supplements in the female's diet, give the animals plenty of heat, bright light and

Above: *Although this frilled lizard is too young to sex with certainty, the femoral pores are beginning to show.*

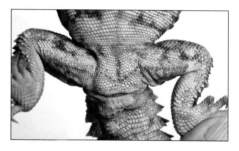

Above: *Although this female Saharan, or Geyr's, Dab Lizard (Uromastyx geyri) has femoral pores, they are smaller than those of males and lack the waxy secretions.*

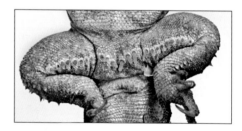

Above: *The femoral pores of this male Eyed Dab Lizard (Uromastyx ocellata) are secreting a waxy substance, used to mark their territory.*

Bearded dragon body language

Watching a group of bearded dragons interact is fascinating. If a group grows up together, a social hierarchy, or 'pecking order', develops with dominant and submissive individuals. As long as there is plenty of space and food, this is not normally a cause for concern; it is natural behaviour and the group as a whole functions better once everybody knows their place.

However, submissive lizards occasionally become so stressed and bullied that they stop feeding, or feed very little, and their growth rate starts to fall behind that of the rest of the group. This usually happens if the enclosure is too small, if the basking spot is too small, if the animals are given insufficient food or if they have nowhere to hide. As a last resort, you will have to set up another enclosure for the smallest lizard and rear it separately, returning it to the group in the original enclosure at a later date once it matches them more closely in size.

Dominance is usually maintained by body language rather than aggression. Bearded dragons lift one or other of their front limbs and wave them in circling movements. This is a sign of recognition in youngsters and submission in older individuals. Females usually arm-wave to males and small males may arm-wave to larger ones if they are in the same enclosure. Head-nodding is a territorial display performed by males to attract females or warn off other males. It can be quite vigorous and the male's colours are often enhanced when it displays. Mating may follow shortly afterwards. When head-nodding occurs between two males of roughly equal size it may escalate. The two lizards square up to each other, flatten their bodies and tilt them towards one another. One may make a dash for the other and grab its neck before trying to press it to the ground in a form of enforced submission. These skirmishes usually end quite quickly and without physical injury. It is simply one lizard's way of showing another one who's boss in the group.

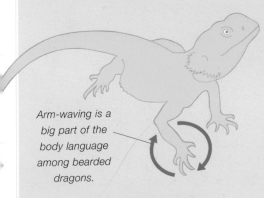

Arm-waving is a big part of the body language among bearded dragons.

Above: A wild Green Garden Lizard (Calotes calotes) laying her eggs in a burrow she has dug in sandy soil at the base of some shrubs.

UV-B, and the lizards will do the rest themselves. If they do not, make sure you really do have at least one male and at least one female. (This may seem obvious, but you would be surprised how many breeding projects fail to get off the ground because of this simple mistake.)

Females that have mated successfully will start to swell with eggs within a few weeks and they will also bask more. Although there is usually a period of four weeks or more between mating and egg laying, it is a good idea to get ready for the clutch before this.

You will need a laying box, a container for the eggs and an incubator. Be sure to set these up well in advance of the expected laying date.

Egg laying

Female bearded dragons normally lay their eggs in burrows in sand or soil, digging down to a level where the substrate is moist. In captivity you can duplicate these conditions by placing a large container of sandy soil or potting compost in the cage. It should be at least 20cm deep and big enough for the female to sit in completely. A plastic storage box measuring about 45cm long, 30cm wide and 30cm deep, with about half the lid cut away, is ideal.

The soil must be moist but not waterlogged. The best way to achieve the right moisture is to soak it well, then tilt the container and squeeze out as much water as you can, leaving moist soil that will support a burrow. Once the female finds a suitable place for her eggs she will begin to dig trial burrows and eventually makes a nest to her satisfaction and lays. Young females lay small clutches of 10 to 15 eggs, but as they grow so does their clutch size. Large females can lay more than 30 eggs and 40 is not unheard of.

After laying, the female covers the nest with soil and levels it. She takes no further part in the incubation and you can safely remove the box from the enclosure. Give the female plenty to eat and drink and make sure she has access to calcium, as she may begin forming another clutch of eggs almost immediately, and lay again in four to six weeks.

Incubating the eggs

Once the female has finished laying, remove the laying box from the enclosure and carefully excavate the nest. You can pick the eggs up carefully with your fingers or use a spoon or scoop. The eggs typically measure about 2-3cm in length and are oval in shape, but there

EGG LAYING BOX

An egg laying box can be as simple as a plastic tub with part of its lid removed.

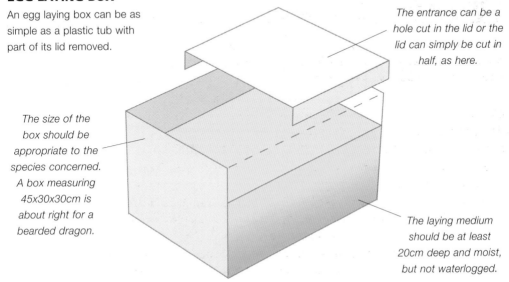

The entrance can be a hole cut in the lid or the lid can simply be cut in half, as here.

The size of the box should be appropriate to the species concerned. A box measuring 45x30x30cm is about right for a bearded dragon.

The laying medium should be at least 20cm deep and moist, but not waterlogged.

is often great variation, even within the same clutch. As they absorb water during their development they swell and become larger and more rounded in shape.

Incubate the eggs in a moist medium such as vermiculite. A fairly coarse grade is best as it allows plenty of air to circulate around the buried part of the egg. Place the vermiculite in a plastic box, such as a freezer box or a clean food container, whose size will depend on the number of eggs. Some breeders use perlite with good success and others use a mixture of vermiculite and perlite – it probably does not matter very much either way. However, getting the moisture right is important. Before adding the eggs you should flood the medium and then leave it at least an hour until it has absorbed all the water it can, then drain off any surplus. Use a minimum of 6cm of medium so that if excess water does collect at the bottom of the container it is well away from the eggs.

Some breeders make a few small holes near the bottom of the box so that excess water can drain away. However, this is not an exact science and as long as the medium is moist but not wet, the eggs should hatch successfully.

The box needs a lid, but it must be ventilated with a few small holes. It is also a good idea to open the box every few days, just for a few seconds, to allow fresh air in. As well as moisture, the eggs need oxygen, especially towards the end of the incubation period.

Each box should contain only the eggs from

Above: Inland Bearded Dragon (Pogona vitticeps) eggs in vermiculite. Note how they are resting in shallow depressions. Although one egg is beginning to discolour, it may well hatch. Do not be in too much of a hurry to discard such eggs, because the shell contains antibacterial and antifungal chemicals to prevent the infection from penetrating to the inside.

one clutch and, wherever possible, try to get the whole clutch in a single box or, at the most, two boxes. This will make monitoring the eggs, and record-keeping, easier.

Place the eggs in the medium separately so that they are not touching one another. They should be partially buried and the easiest way to arrange them is to make a series of impressions in the substrate with your thumb then place one egg in each. Do not make the impressions too close together because the eggs will swell during the incubation period. Put the lid on the box and write the date, number of eggs and which female laid them if you have more than one female. Put the box in the incubator, having first checked that the temperature is set correctly.

Do not turn the eggs during incubation and avoid disturbing them in any way. Do not spray them; if the medium seems to be drying out, run a small amount of water down the inside of the box. If any eggs start to shrivel, grow mould, become slimy, smell or generally look 'unhealthy'

be prepared to remove them. Good eggs rarely become seriously infested with mould, but often become slightly discoloured and this is nothing to worry about.

Preparing the incubator

The eggs need a temperature of 28-30°C and this must be controlled with a thermostat. You can make an incubator out of a wooden cabinet or polystyrene box or buy a small poultry

A BASIC INCUBATOR

An incubator needs to be set up in advance so that the temperature has time to settle down. It can be adapted cheaply from a polystyrene fish box, although serious breeders prefer to use one that has been built especially for the purpose.

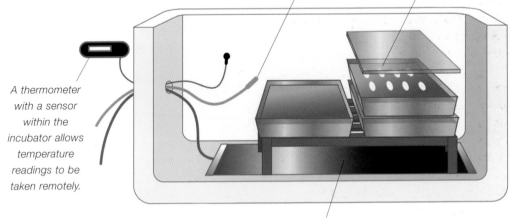

A thermostat sensor attached to one side, about half way up.

Shallow plastic boxes with eggs resting in a substrate of vermiculite.

A thermometer with a sensor within the incubator allows temperature readings to be taken remotely.

A heat mat on the floor of the incubator. This should not be in contact with the egg boxes, which can be raised on upturned, empty boxes or on a rack made from dowelling rods.

incubator. Home-made incubators should be up and running several days, or even weeks, before the eggs are put in them so that you can check the temperature with a maximum-minimum thermometer. A digital thermometer with a remote probe is the best tool. Place the probe inside the incubator and the read-out outside. Check it frequently and keep resetting the maximum and minimum readouts. Fine-tune the thermostat based on the reading.

Make sure that the temperature is even throughout the incubator by placing the probe in different areas. A temperature that varies by a degree or two is acceptable, but if it varies by more than this you may have to redesign the incubator. Heat pads or heat strips are the best way to provide heat.

Good air circulation is important to avoid hot or cold spots, so shelves, for instance, should be made of perforated material or slats and should stop short of the front and back of the unit.

Hatching

This is one of the most enthralling parts of breeding reptiles; even after many years of breeding, and incubating hundreds of clutches of eggs, nothing compares to looking in the

Below: Towards the end of the incubation period check the box every day and remove any hatchlings. Otherwise, they will disturb the eggs yet to hatch. These are hatchling Inland Bearded Dragons; their discarded shells are still visible.

incubator to find that hatchlings have appeared. Towards the end of the incubation period – the last few days – the eggs may begin to collapse as the baby lizards use up the yolk and fluid. Do not panic! This is normal and you should see slits appearing in the eggshells shortly after this. In the case of bearded dragons, all the eggs should hatch within a day or two. Any that do not may contain dead embryos, but do not be in too much of a hurry to dispose of them because sometimes there are stragglers, especially if the temperature across the

Right: *Newly hatched Inland Bearded Dragons are fully formed miniatures of their parents and will soon start exploring.*

Temperature-dependent sex determination

In crocodilians, turtles and some lizards, the sexes of offspring are not determined by sex chromosomes, as they are in most animals, but by the temperature at which their eggs are incubated, particularly at a point about one-third through the incubation period. This is known as temperature-dependent sex determination (TSD). In the lizards that have been studied so far, such as leopard geckos, low temperatures in the early stages of incubation result in females, whereas higher temperatures result in males. Some *breeders have noticed a skewed sex ratio in bearded dragons when eggs are incubated at particularly high or low temperatures, but the results are inconclusive; they could just as easily be caused by chance. At present, then, there is no scientific evidence that bearded dragons' sexes are determined by the temperature at which their eggs are incubated. However, in the case of the Red-headed Rock Agama (Agama agama) TSD has been established; indeed, it was one of the first reptiles in which TSD was noticed.*

incubator is not perfectly even. It is best to resist the temptation to slit the eggs with scissors to help the hatchlings out. On the one hand you may slit the shell before the lizard inside is fully developed, which is likely to harm or kill it and, on the other, if the lizard is too weak to slit its own shell it is unlikely to live anyway. It is unrealistic to expect a 100% hatch-rate every time.

Caring for the hatchlings

Hatchlings should be left in the incubation box for several hours after they have hatched. They will be exhausted and a respite in the dark, warm and humid environment will be good for them. Once they become alert and start to run about in the box they can be moved to an enclosure similar to that described for young bearded dragons (see *Housing* page 69). Paper kitchen towels are the best substrate at first. Watch the hatchlings carefully to make sure they are basking

and feeding. A light misting with water is also good for them, but the enclosure must be well ventilated so that humidity does not build up. Within a few days they will learn to associate their owner with food and be ready and waiting at feeding time. Juveniles are very reluctant to take any vegetable material and can be given small sizes of any of the recommended insect species. Be sure to dust each feed with vitamin and mineral supplements (see page 81). Only feed the juveniles as many insects as they can eat in about ten minutes, and feed them twice each day if possible. If they clear up the insects in less than ten minutes, increase the quantity slightly.

If all your eggs hatch, you will end up with a surplus of juveniles. Once you are happy that

Right: *At three months old, these Inland Bearded Dragons are alert and active. Be sure to feed them as recommended.*

they are all healthy and feeding, you may be able to dispose of them to other lizard-keepers, perhaps through a society or breeders' meeting, or to a local pet store. Many breeders like to hold back a few of their own offspring and, if you gradually thin them out as they grow, you can often select the strongest and most colourful individuals for possible future breeding stock.

Selective breeding

Simply put, selective breeding means selecting the best animals as future breeders and mating them together. 'Best' might mean the largest, most vigorous or most colourful. Many breeders develop lines or strains of bearded dragons that perpetuate a colour form that crops up unexpectedly

in captivity, whereas others work on strains that are naturally colourful and strive to improve their colour even more. The simplest way of selectively breeding a species is to match the best male with the best female but, as these will often be related to each other (sometimes brother and sister) this is not a good long-term plan. Fresh stock must be introduced to inject some hybrid vigour into the strain every two or three generations, otherwise it will deteriorate.

The first rule of selective breeding is to select healthy animals, even if they are not the most colourful. Using runty or deformed stock just because they have a particularly desirable colour or pattern is not the way to proceed. Assuming,

Above: At eight months you can begin to assess your bearded dragons for breeding, although wait until they are at least 12 to 18 months old.

105

however, that your desirable lizard is strong and healthy, but you prefer not to mate it to a close relative, you can 'out-cross' it to an unrelated individual. This will inject some genetic variation into the strain.

Depending on the trait, you may find that all the offspring look normal, and not at all like the ones you were hoping to produce. This is because many of the desirable traits are carried on recessive genes which, when paired with matching genes from another individual, are not expressed. Do not despair, the characteristic you are interested in will still be there and, in order to see its effect, you need to mate one or more of the offspring (which are, in effect, 'carriers' of the gene) with another carrier. This can be another lizard from the same litter (a brother or sister), which will also have one normal gene and one hidden gene, or with the parent that has the trait, and which will have two of the desirable genes.

Mating an offspring to one of its parents is known as 'back-crossing' and will result, statistically, in equal numbers of normal-looking and 'desirable' genes. Mating an offspring with a brother or sister gives a less satisfactory result: one quarter

'desirable', one quarter normal and one half that look normal, but that are also carrying the 'desirable' gene. These latter are called heterozygous animals, usually shortened to 'heteros'. Heterozygous animals are indistinguishable from normal ones and can only be identified by further breeding trials.

At other times, out-crossing results in offspring that show a mixture of characteristics, including some that are close to the type you are trying to produce. By breeding two of these together you can gradually improve your strain over two or three generations before needing to out-cross again.

Left: A Leucistic morph. The bone coloured scales and pigmented eyes are typical of this morph.

***Above:** A Canary Yellow Tiger Hypo Translucent Smoothie morph.*

BREEDING STRATEGY

This diagram traces how dominant and recessive genes are passed on and control the albino characteristic in successive generations of bearded dragons. Heterozygous individuals look normal but have one dominant and one recessive gene.

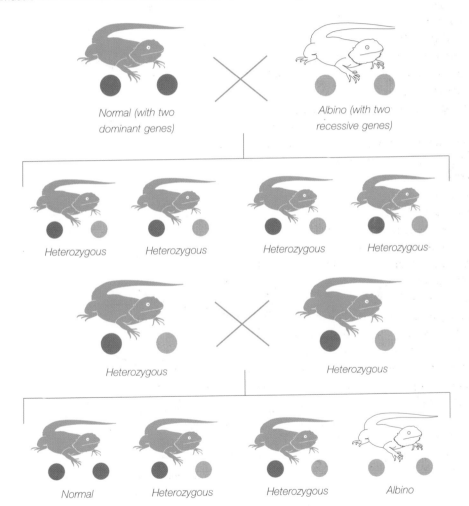

Normal (with two dominant genes)

Albino (with two recessive genes)

Heterozygous

Heterozygous

Heterozygous

Heterozygous

Heterozygous

Heterozygous

Normal

Heterozygous

Heterozygous

Albino

In this section we deal mainly with the different types of bearded dragons, but we also look at a number of other attractive lizards that are sometimes available. However, most of these species are rarely bred in captivity, so caring for them presents certain problems that you are unlikely

to encounter with bearded dragons. Some of these animals are large and active and require very large enclosures and all need careful attention to their diets, including supplements, if they are to stay healthy.

Part Two

SPECIES PROFILES

BEARDED DRAGONS, FRILLED
LONG-TAILED
EARLESS DRAGONS

LIZARDS AND

Above: *An Orange Translucent morph of the Inland Bearded Dragon.*

Left: *A Frilled Lizard* (Chlamydosaurus kingii) *in full display.*

Of the six species of bearded dragons, two – the Inland, or Central, Bearded Dragon and Rankin's Bearded Dragon – are kept in captivity on a regular basis. The Inland Bearded Dragon *(Pogona vitticeps)* is by far the commonest species and all the various colour forms, or morphs, in the pet trade belong to this species.

Frilled Lizards all belong to the same species, *Chlamydosaurus kingii*. They are large, distinctive lizards, famous for their large frill, or ruff, which they spread when they are displaying. They make popular pets and are bred in captivity on a regular basis. Juveniles are more expensive than bearded dragons as they are rarer and, as they grow, they require large enclosures because they need to climb.

The Long-tailed Earless Dragon *(Tympanocryptis tetraporophora)* is smaller than bearded dragons. The generic name means 'hidden ear'; although they do have ears, these are hidden by a flap of scaly skin. In many ways, their lifestyle is similar to that of the African agama lizards and their captive care is similar as a result.

Inland, or Central, Bearded Dragon

Pogona vitticeps is the most familiar species of bearded dragon. It measures 250mm SVL, 450mm TL. The normal, or 'wild-type', bearded dragon has a sandy or brown pattern on a lighter background, a row of pointed spines along the flanks and another series of spines across the back of the head. The 'beard' is a well-developed patch of pointed scales on the throat, which are erected when the lizard displays. These scales are often dark grey or black but are sometimes reddish. Captive dragons rarely display fully, although they sometimes puff out their throats momentarily when they interact with one another (or in response to a perceived threat, such as a dog, cat or human they are not familiar with). The markings on the back are sometimes arranged into wide, irregular light and dark bands and there are often dark markings radiating out from the eyes. The facial markings are sometimes flushed with orange.

The Rankin's Bearded Dragon (see page 120) is a similar species.

Availability

P. vitticeps is readily available in a wide variety of colour forms and at all ages.

Life in the wild

Inland Bearded Dragons live in dry woodlands in the interior of Australia, often climbing onto fence posts, dead stumps and tree trunks to bask and to survey their surroundings. They feed on a wide variety of prey, including insects and small vertebrates, such as small snakes and lizards, and also eat some vegetation, including fruit, leaves and flowers. When they feel threatened they face their enemy, open their mouth widely, displaying the bright yellow interior, and extend their beard.

Care in captivity

In captivity they are calm and deliberate in their movements, making them ideal display animals. They are willing to be handled and some individuals seem to enjoy handling,

especially if there is a chance of a favourite food: they particularly relish waxworms and giant mealworms, which can be used to 'bribe' them, but offer these foods sparingly as they are not an ideal diet. For more advice see pages 76-85.

Below: A juvenile wild-type Inland Bearded Dragon, showing the bold markings typical of this species during the first few months of its life.

The dark lines radiating from the eyes are more clearly seen in juveniles than adults.

Below: An adult wild-type Inland Bearded Dragon, in which the bold juvenile markings have faded, so that the lizard has an almost uniform coloration.

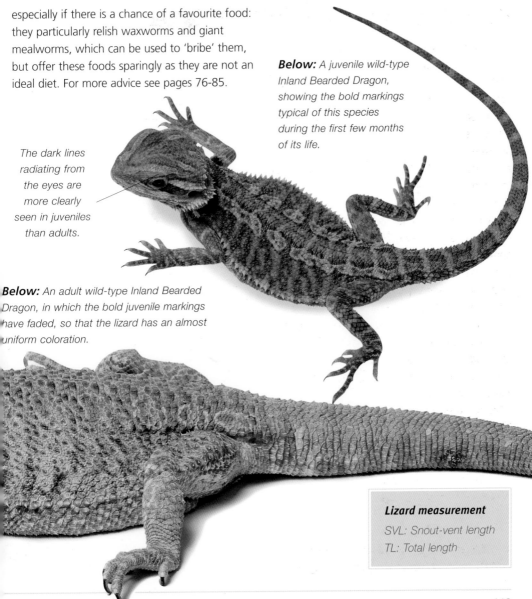

Lizard measurement

SVL: Snout-vent length

TL: Total length

113

Morphs of the Inland Bearded Dragon

One of the main attractions of bearded dragons, apart from the ease with which they can be kept and bred in captivity and their calm temperament, is the wide variety of morphs available on the market. These range from

selecting the most colourful or attractive individuals from a batch of offspring and breeds them together, the aim being to 'fix' and, if possible, to enhance the colour. The best offspring from the second generation are then selected as further breeding stock and so on. Occasional out-breedings are necessary to prevent genetic problems

animals with enhanced coloration produced by methodical selective breeding to the unusual and (sometimes) wonderful creations of imaginative breeders (see also page 105).

There are three basic ways in which these colour forms, or morphs, can be produced.

Selective breeding occurs when a breeder makes use of natural variation in colour by

(inbreeding) and the process can take many generations. Sometimes individuals from a wild population are more colourful than normal and these can give the breeder a head start but, in the case of bearded dragons, which cannot

Below: *A Yellow-red Desert morph of the Inland Bearded Dragon, a form in which the yellow coloration is particularly extensive and bright.*

Note the bright yellow coloration on the beard of this specimen.

be legally exported from their country of origin (Australia) this is not an option. Despite this, some of the first bloodlines of colourful bearded dragons that appeared in the 1980s and 1990s are thought to have originated in this way.

Genetic mutations sometimes occur in any breeding programme, and the more animals that are produced the higher the likelihood of something 'interesting' cropping up. Albino animals – individuals that lack pigment and have pink eyes – are a good example of this and albinos seem to occur in practically every species of animal, including wild populations.

Other common mutations among bearded dragons include leucistic individuals (animals that are pale, like albinos, but have dark eyes), amelanistic individuals (animals that lack the pigment melanin, which produces black and brown markings), and hypomelanistic individuals (animals that have a reduced amount of melanin and whose markings are pale and washed out). In amelanistic and hypomelanistic animals, any other colours that may be present, such as orange, yellow, etc., are often stronger because they are no longer masked by the darker pigment. Other naturally occurring

Below: An Orange Translucent morph of the Inland Bearded Dragon, a form in which the outer scales lack some of their normal white pigment, allowing the underlying orange pigment to show through.

mutations include forms with reduced scalation, or which lack scales altogether.

Genetic breeding programmes aim to 'create' new morphs by breeding animals of different genetic types. These can be selectively bred animals or animals that have a colour or scale mutation, or one selectively bred animal with a mutant form. For example, mating a dragon that has been selectively bred for bright coloration with one that is hypomelanistic will produce offspring that have little black or brown pigment, but are well endowed with orange pigment.

As more forms arise, whatever their origin, the possibilities of crossing different types expands exponentially, so that there is an almost endless number of permutations. Animals of some types are highly sought-after and fetch high prices but, as pets, they are no better than the standard bearded dragons that are similar to those found in the wild. Many morphs have names, some of them quite fanciful, but the descriptions can be subjective so buyers are advised to see the stock from which they are buying. This is especially important if high prices are involved, as juveniles often do not show

Colour forms (it is not possible to list them all and most are self-explanatory)

Hypo short for hypomelanistic. This is a genetic trait, controlled by recessive genes and not subject to variation. Hypomelanistic dragons have reduced dark pigmentation and colourless claws.

Leucistic is another genetic trait, controlled by recessive genes. Leucistic dragons are pale, almost white, in colour but have dark eyes. Selectively bred leucistic dragons with little or no pattern are sometimes marketed as 'Snow' dragons.

'Pastel' dragons are hypomelanistic and have been selectively bred for colour, resulting in an attractive

their bright colours until they are approaching sexual maturity. The more reputable breeders provide a certificate with the animal, describing its morph along with details of its parentage and date of hatching.

The following are some of the more established types:

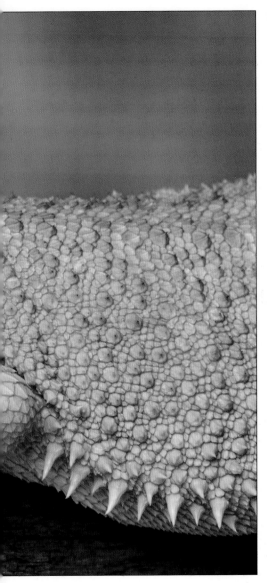

pastel coloration, such as yellow, orange, etc. The lack of dark pigment allows underlying colours to show through.

'Translucent' dragons lack some of the white pigment that is normally beneath the surface of their scales, giving them a translucent appearance and allowing other pigments to show.

'Sunset', 'Flame', 'Tangerine', 'Peach', etc. are all subjective colour descriptions of various strains. All of these can be combined with other forms, such as leucistic, hypomelanistic, etc.

'Tiger' dragons with a pattern arranged into definite transverse bands.

'Patternless' dragons have lost all traces of pattern.

Scalation abnormalities

'Leatherback' dragons lack the random large tubercles scattered among the scales of wild individuals.

'Smoothies' are similar to leatherbacks but arose independently in a different bloodline.

'Silkbacks' are like leatherbacks but lack all scales, including the spines that run along their flanks and those on the throat forming the beard. They are considered to be more delicate than leatherbacks and other types because their skin is not protected.

Left: The Canary Yellow Tiger Hypo lizard has reduced dark pigment, enhanced yellow coloration and a banded dorsal pattern (not visible here).

Rankin's Bearded Dragon

The common name of this species is something of a mystery. In Australia it is more usually called the Downs Bearded Dragon, and in North America it is sometimes called Lawson's Bearded Dragon. There is a genus of agamids in Australia called *Rankinia*, but these are nothing to do with Rankin's dragons.

Pogona henrylawsoni measures up to 150mm SVL, 240mm TL and is significantly smaller than the Inland Bearded Dragon (*P. vitticeps*). Compared with *P. vitticeps*, Rankin's beard is less well developed, its head is proportionately smaller and more rounded and lacks the row of large pointed spines at the back. The spines along its flanks are also smaller. It is pale yellowish-brown in colour with two rows of pale blotches down its back, one on each side of the midline. Its behaviour is similar to that of the inland bearded dragon.

Availability

This species is available in small numbers. For reasons that are not clear, it does not appear to breed as readily in captivity as its larger relative.

Life in the wild

Rankin's Bearded Dragon occurs over a much smaller area than *P. vitticeps* in central Queensland, Australia, where its habitat is grassy clay plains, with few trees.

Similar species

The Common, or Eastern, Bearded Dragon (Pogona barbata) may be bred in small quantities but is not freely available. There have been reports of hybrids between Rankin's Bearded Dragons and Inland Bearded Dragons, marketed under the made-up name of 'Vittikin' dragons. They are unlikely to offer any advantages over the two 'pure' species and are probably best avoided.

Care in captivity

This species makes a good pet and its care is exactly as for the Inland Bearded Dragon. However, being smaller, it does not require such a large vivarium. It will live harmoniously in small groups consisting of a male and one or more females. It becomes tame and is long-lived. Better supplies of captive-bred stock would be welcome.

At the time of writing there do not appear to be any colour morphs of this species.

Right: An adult Rankin's Bearded Dragon (Pogona henrylawsoni) in which the characteristic rounded snout and reduced spines at the back of the head are clear to see.

Frilled Lizard

Chlamydosaurus kingii is a long, slender species with a long tail. It measures 250mm SVL, 600-700mm TL. Its most obvious characteristic, and the one that renders it unmistakable, is the large flap of loose skin attached to its neck. When at rest, the frill is folded over the lizard's shoulders like a cape and it is only erected if the lizard senses danger. Then it will face its enemy and open out the frill like an umbrella. The frill itself can measure up to 30cm across and may be grey, orange or reddish in colour. The frills of males are more colourful than those of females. At the same time as it erects its frill, the lizard opens its mouth widely, displaying the bright yellow interior. Captive-raised frilled lizards rarely open out their frill fully unless persuaded to do so by the presence of a predator such as a dog, snake or larger lizard, or by placing a mirror in front of them.

As a defence mechanism, the frill is only used as a last resort if the lizard is cornered. Its first line of defence is to remain motionless on an upright tree trunk or to move slowly around to the far side so that it is hidden from view. If it is caught in the open it runs away rapidly, sometimes raising itself up onto its hind limbs, and makes for a nearby tree to climb.

Availability

Frilled lizards are bred in captivity in North America and Europe. The supply is not plentiful, however, and obtaining captive-bred young can take time. Wild stock is imported from Indonesia occasionally but is of poor quality compared with captive-bred animals. Australian animals are protected by law.

In the wild

The Frilled Lizard occurs in Australasia and New Guinea, but all captive-bred stock appears to have originated in New Guinea.

Care in captivity

These are attractive and fascinating lizards, second only to bearded dragons for the way in which they adapt to captivity. Captive-bred juveniles soon become tame and will approach their owner to be fed. They are easy to handle, although they do have the potential to bite.

Choosing The advice on choosing a bearded dragon (pages 30-36) applies equally to frilled lizards. Captive-bred animals are far preferable to wild-caught ones, which are invariably infested with internal and external parasites. These must be detected, identified and treated at the earliest opportunity. Taking this into account, buying a wild-caught frilled lizard is a false economy,

Right: A wild Australian Frilled Lizard makes itself look bigger and more ferocious by opening its mouth widely and erecting its frill.

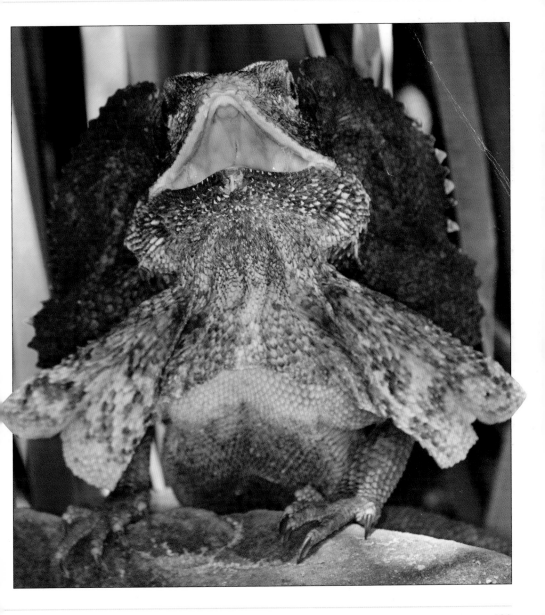

even though it may be older and larger than a captive-bred one of equivalent price. Captive-bred individuals will also adapt better to you and your home and will make much better pets.

Males are more colourful than females and also more active and bolder, giving the impression that they are more extroverted. Males are territorial, so you can only keep one to an enclosure. If you intend to breed frilled lizards, a pair or a group consisting of one male to two females, will live together harmoniously once they have established a pecking order.

Above: *A relatively compact enclosure such as this, with branches and plastic plants, can be used to house several juvenile frilled lizards.*

Housing is the biggest problem, as these large, active lizards must be given an opportunity to climb. Adults need an enclosure with the same floor dimensions as those recommended for bearded dragons (ideally a minimum of 200x60cm) but much taller – at least 150cm. The recommendations relating to cage materials (page 59) apply to this species but, as it requires a higher humidity than bearded dragons, plastic-faced chipboard is less suitable in the long term unless you seal the joints thoroughly with silicon sealant. Provide plenty of opportunities for the lizard(s) to climb. These can range from simple structures made of rough timber to natural logs and branches. The back and sides of the enclosure can be covered with cork bark or cork tiles to provide extra opportunities for climbing. Direct the heating and lighting onto a sloping branch on which the lizards can bask, The advice on pages 45-50 concerning heat and UV-B apply equally to this species.

Bark chippings (orchid bark) make a suitable substrate for the floor of the enclosure, although some keepers prefer sand as it is not as dusty. A mixture of sand and bark chippings in equal amounts can also work well and the recent introduction of coconut fibre, or coir, is another option that can be explored. Either way, it is important to spray the enclosure on a daily basis so that the floor covering can absorb some of the water and release it slowly for the next few hours to raise the humidity slightly. However, you must not allow the enclosure to steam up, so provide adequate ventilation.

Below: A naturalistic vivarium suitable for a pair or trio of adult frilled lizards. The ceramic heater and spiral UV-B lamp provide vital heat and light.

Feeding Unlike bearded dragons, frilled lizards do not eat vegetation as a rule, although they may ingest small quantities incidentally with their food. Hatchlings and juveniles will eat crickets and locusts, as well as any other insects you can obtain and which make a welcome addition to their diet. Waxworms and mealworms can be given in moderation. Meals must be dusted with vitamin and mineral supplements. As the animals grow, they can be offered young mice that have been thoroughly thawed out, but insects should continue to be the main diet.

Below: A clutch of frilled lizard eggs, partially buried in a vermiculite substrate. The eggs have been lightly marked on their upper surface so that they can be replaced the right way up if they are moved for any reason.

Adult frilled lizards will eat adult mice as well as large locusts, giant mealworms and adult crickets. They also eat smaller lizards in the wild; this species is not welcome in a community enclosure and only individuals of similar size can be housed together.

Breeding Frilled lizards will breed in captivity provided their environment is correct. Firstly, the enclosure must be large enough for the various displays and interactions to take place. The animals must be well conditioned, so feed them a varied diet supplemented with vitamins and minerals. Breeding behaviour can be stimulated by spraying the enclosure to raise the humidity after the animals have been kept dry for several weeks. An increase in day length may also be necessary, going from twelve to sixteen hours each day, increased gradually over three or four weeks. This regime will stimulate the male to become more territorial and to display more frequently.

Mating takes place several times and stops only when the female(s) contains developing eggs. As her body starts to swell with eggs she will begin to search for a suitable egg-laying site. This should be a deep container of peat, sand or a peat-sand mixture, kept damp but not waterlogged.

Clutches usually number fewer than ten eggs, although females can lay several times in a single season. Remove the eggs from the enclosure and incubate them artificially as described on page

Above: A frilled lizard egg in the early stages of hatching. The hatchling has pushed its snout through the shell, but may take several more hours to emerge completely.

99-102. At 28°C they hatch after about three months. As is usual with reptiles, all the eggs hatch within a day or two of each other. The hatchlings will start to move around after one or two more days and begin to bask and feed within about one week of hatching.

Rearing the young is straightforward, providing you follow the advice on maintaining a suitable environment and supplement their diet with vitamins and minerals. They require more frequent spraying than adults. Maintain a moderately high humidity, but with good ventilation. Small groups of frilled lizards can be raised together in a large glass or plastic vivarium, although as the animals grow they will require increasing amounts of space. Most breeders dispose of surplus young once they are feeding and growing well, and keep back only enough to ensure another generation of breeding adults.

Determining the sexes of hatchlings is very difficult but, as they approach maturity, males grow more quickly than females and eventually reach a greater size. In addition, their frills are larger and more showy and they are more inclined to display. Males also develop a pair of hemipenal bulges (see page 94). It may be possible for an experienced veterinarian to sex young frilled lizards by everting the hemipenes ('popping'), but inexperienced keepers should not attempt to do this.

Above: A young frilled lizard looking around its enclosure. The frill is folded beneath its neck.

Long-tailed Earless Dragon

All eight of the Australian earless dragons are plump lizards with broad heads and slender tails. They measure 74mm SVL, 150mm TL. Their scales are small, but there are clusters of larger, spiny scales scattered over their bodies. Their common name arises from the apparent lack of a tympanum, or eardrum, which is in fact present, but covered by scaly skin. Earless dragons somewhat resemble juvenile Rankin's dragons and are also superficially similar in appearance to the larger African ground agamas and the Middle-Eastern Toad-headed Agamas (*Phrynocephalus* species). Do not confuse them with the American Earless Lizard (*Holbrookia* species), a member of the Phrynosomatidae, and more closely related to iguanas.

Tympanocryptis tetraporophora has variable coloration but is often reddish brown with darker blotches down its back, sometimes forming a series of irregular cross-bars. Its tail is barred dark and light brown.

Males display by head-bobbing and by inflating their bodies but they are less aggressive than other dragon lizards.

Availability

Tympanocryptis tetraporophora is the species most commonly kept in captivity, although at least one other species, *T. lineata*, may also be kept in small numbers.

Other species of earless dragons may be available; if so, they will be in short supply as these are Australian species that cannot be legally collected and exported. As they are all similar in appearance and behaviour, other species can be kept and bred under similar conditions.

Life in the wild

The Long-tailed Earless Dragon is a fast-moving, heat-seeking lizard, found in some of the most ferociously hot parts of the central Australian

Above: *The Long-tailed Earless Dragon is proving adaptable in captivity and breeding regularly.*

desert. It lives in open habitats on gravel plains and sparse woodland.

Care in captivity

T. tetraporophora is fairly new to the hobby but it looks promising.

Housing Because of its small size and lack of aggression, small groups can be kept together in colonies. Enclosures measuring 80-100cm long and 40-50cm wide are sufficient for a group of two to four animals. Height is of little

Above: This female is showing obvious signs of being gravid. She may lay up to eight eggs, although four to six is a more usual number.

importance provided they cannot escape and there is room for a basking lamp. Place this at one end of the enclosure with a pile of rocks beneath it. The temperature under the lamp should be at least 40°C throughout the day and of a type that also gives off UV-B. Alternatively, use separate lamps for heating and lighting as described on page 53. Bear in mind that smaller

enclosures require less powerful UV-B lamps, but the distance from the lamp to the basking place should be a maximum of 30cm to ensure that the lizards benefit.

Feeding Long-tailed earless dragons are insectivores and will eat most cultured live foods, such as crickets, locusts and mealworms, which should be dusted with a vitamin and mineral supplement. They are active hunters and food can be scattered around the enclosure for them to chase. There is no evidence that they eat leaves or other vegetation but there is no harm

Above: This female Long-tailed Earless Dragon will lay her eggs in the next few days. She will need somewhere suitable to bury the eggs.

in trying. (If indeed they refuse plant material, there could be an opportunity here to plant out the enclosure with some well-chosen succulents to make it more interesting.)

Breeding is regularly achieved. *T. tetraporophora* can reach breeding size in six to twelve months, and males can be distinguished from females by the presence of four pores on their thighs, two on each side. Their behaviour also differs as they will display to the females and other males and chase and mate with females. Gravid females are easily recognised when they swell with eggs; place a laying box in the enclosure at this time. The box should contain 15cm of damp peat-sand mixture with a piece of flat slate or bark covering part of the surface. Alternatively provide a box with a lid into which an aperture has been cut. The essential factor is that the substrate should retain some moisture and not dry out

Below: Hatchling Long-tailed Earless Dragons breaking out of their eggs. The eggs were moved to a substrate of damp vermiculite as soon as they were laid so that they could be incubated under constant conditions of temperature and humidity.

too quickly. The animals lay up to eight eggs per clutch and will produce eggs every four weeks if well fed and given plenty of calcium.

The eggs hatch in about 50 days at 28°C and the hatchlings measure a mere 25mm in total length. They are best housed in a clean plastic container with paper towelling or clean sand and sprayed daily to prevent dehydration; in the wild, breeding is timed to coincide with the rainy season. Offer small live food straight away, such as hatchling crickets or the next size up, after they have moulted once (known as first instar), aphids and small waxworms. The youngsters can be moved to a set-up similar to that of the adults by the time they are four to eight weeks old. Sex determination is not possible until they reach adult size.

FOREST AND
WATER DRAGONS

The forest and water dragons occur in the rainforests of Southeast Asia and Australasia. They are medium-sized to large lizards that tend to be well camouflaged in shades of green, olive and brown and their usual strategy is to remain motionless and hope to escape the notice of predators. In captivity this behaviour lends itself to naturalistic displays, as they will often remain on show when other lizards would run away and hide.

All forest and water dragons need large enclosures, tall enough to allow the animals to behave naturally. Some species – the so-called water dragons – are semi-aquatic and require large containers of water in which to bathe. All species require a humid environment, but their temperature requirements are lower than those of bearded dragons and other agamas. Similarly, their exposure to UV-B is not as great under natural conditions and it is to be expected that they need less of this in captivity than the other species. However, exact requirements in this respect have not been properly studied.

Above: A Thai Water Dragon (Physignathus cocincinus). This lizard breeds readily in captivity.

Left: The agile, arboreal Green Crested Lizard (Bronchocela cristatella) is a typical example of the forest dragons of Asia and Australasia.

Armoured Prickle-nape Agama

Acanthosaura armata is a Southeast Asian forest dragon measuring 140mm SVL, 300mm TL. Its unusual crest consists of very long, needlelike scales running down its back and it also has a pair of pointed scales over its eyes. It is greenish brown in colour, with indistinct spots and cross bands, and the throat and face are flushed with yellow and orange. Adult males are more slender, have higher crests, and are usually more colourful than females.

Availability

It is imported occasionally but not widely bred.

Life in the wild

This dragon lizard relies heavily on camouflage to escape detection. It rests motionless on tree trunks and branches, even when closely approached. However, if it breaks cover, it can run quickly and after covering several metres it freezes again.

Care in captivity

Because most specimens will be imported from the wild, be sure to take the usual precautions regarding diseases, parasites and quarantine.

A. armata is a calm species provided it has a secluded enclosure with plenty of natural places to rest. When approached or handled it may open its mouth widely, displaying the bright orange interior, but soon adapts to captivity.

Housing *A. armata* needs a tall enclosure, at least one metre high, preferably higher, stocked with upright or slightly sloping branches on which to rest. It looks most at home on moss-covered branches, where its colours and markings help it to blend in. Tropical plants, such as *Philodendron* species, can be kept in the enclosure, preferably in their pots. The lizards, being slow-moving and not easily stressed, will not normally damage them.

A hot-spot towards the top of the enclosure should provide a temperature of around 25-30°C, but there should be ample opportunities for the lizard to retreat into the shade. Provide UV-B at low levels and subdued overall lighting. Daily spraying is essential and this can be done with an automatic system.

Feeding This insectivorous species will eat the usual range of crickets, locusts and waxworms, which should be dusted with supplements. It is particularly fond of earthworms.

Breeding has been achieved in Germany and possibly elsewhere. The male displays by head-

Right: The Armoured Prickle-nape Agama from Southeast Asia (Acanthosaura armata) *is one of the more spectacular species. Males in particular have long spines over their eyes and along their back.*

bobbing and biting, after which mating takes place. The female lays 10-15 eggs, which she buries, so place a suitable nesting box filled with a sand-peat mixture into the enclosure in preparation.

At 25°C the eggs hatch after about 190 days and the newly hatched young are 7cm in length. They require similar conditions to the adults, but should be kept in a separate enclosure to prevent the possibility of cannibalism.

Below: An Armoured Prickle-nape Agama in the wild. This species can thrive in captivity, but needs a naturalistic vivarium with plenty of hiding places and humid conditions.

Similar species

The Mountain Prickle-nape Agama (Acanthosaura capra) is sometimes imported but information is sparse. It is smaller than the Armoured Prickle-nape and its crest is shorter and not as impressive. The 'thorns' over its eyes are shorter and curved. Judging from its native habitat in Cambodia and Vietnam, it requires a moderate temperature and high humidity. Imported females are sometimes gravid and lay their eggs shortly after arrival. Incubation is as for A. armata. The hatchlings are about 7cm TL and more active than the adults.

The Brown Prickle-nape (A. lepidogaster) has been imported from Vietnam, and there are several other species in the genus that could, potentially, appear in the pet trade. A good starting point for keeping these interesting lizards would be to keep them in the same way as the Armoured Prickle-nape, but to be prepared to adjust parameters such as heating, lighting and diet as necessary. Again, note the precautions necessary when buying wild-caught lizards. Animals of this type should only be attempted by experienced keepers.

Mountain Horned Dragon

Acanthosaura crucigera, from Southeast Asia, is similar in many respects to *A. armata*, but is more slender and its crest is not as tall. It measures 120mm SVL, 300mm TL. The toothlike scales on the neck are separated from those on the back by a small gap, and the crest becomes gradually lower until it almost disappears entirely at a point between the front and back limbs. Males have long spines over their eyes, but females lack these and are smaller than males. This species is usually brown or olive but changes colour according to mood. When it is warm it becomes paler. Males develop a black collar during the breeding season, but at other times their markings are indistinct. The prominent eye is brilliant russet-orange. Like *A. armata*, this species relies on its camouflage and tends to remain motionless most of the time.

Availability

It is occasionally imported, but rarely available captive-bred.

Care in captivity

This is a relatively easy species to keep in captivity. However, it is easily stressed and must have a large, tall enclosure, with vertical branches on which to climb. Plenty of cover, in the form of leaves – either natural or artificial – will go a long way towards helping the animals settle in. They will not damage living plants,

provided these are fairly tough varieties, such as *Philodendron* species. They like to soak and will spend long periods of time submerged if they have a sufficiently large water container; a semi-aquatic set-up (a paludarium) would probably suit them well. They prefer lower temperatures of about 20°C during the day and slightly cooler conditions at night. Provide a basking lamp, but it is important to ensure that it does not cause the temperature throughout the enclosure to rise too much; a low-power spotlight is the best arrangement. Otherwise, lighting, feeding, etc., are as for the previous species, but it is not advisable to keep both species together.

Breeding has been achieved, but is rarely attempted. The male displays to the female by vigorous head-bobbing, but females will reject males aggressively if they are not ready to mate or if they are already gravid. Injuries can occur and, in general, it is better to house the animals individually, except at breeding time, unless a very large enclosure can be provided. Gravid females need a substrate of peat and sand in which to bury their eggs, which they lay about 50 days after mating.

Right: The Mountain Horned Dragon is a medium-sized forest dragon that tames down well in captivity. It requires cooler conditions than many of its relatives.

Green Crested Lizard

Bronchocela cristatella is a beautiful agamid from Southeast Asia. This slender lizard has very long, thin limbs and a long tail and measures 120mm SVL, 500mm TL. Its overall green colour varies from yellowish-green to blue-green, with a scattering of small, white or pale blue spots on its side. It has a crest of enlarged scales; these are higher in males than females, and males have a small throat fan.

Availability

Wild imported animals from Southeast Asia are occasionally available, but this species is not widely bred in captivity.

Life in the wild

B. cristatella occurs in a variety of habitats, including gardens and parks. This highly arboreal species climbs into leafy shrubs, where it is difficult to see unless it moves. When resting on vertical branches it typically holds its body away from the surface.

Care in captivity

This is not a species for beginners. It requires high humidity but good airflow, and a large, thickly planted enclosure. Without opportunities

Right: The Green Crested Lizard is a colourful and wide-ranging forest dragon, found from India to Southeast Asia, photographed here in Borneo.

to hide among foliage it will soon become stressed and die. It needs a temperature of at least 25°C but 28-35°C is better. A temperature drop of about 10°C at night is required and a source of UV-B is essential.

B. cristatella will eat most of the commonly

available insect foods, such as crickets and waxworms. Provide as wide a variety of foods as possible. Spray the vivarium at least once each day, or use an automatic sprinkler system, as this species is reluctant to drink from a bowl.

Females lay one or two elongated eggs, which hatch after 60 to 70 days at 30°C. Captive breeding is a rare event.

Similar species

The genus includes five other species from Southeast Asia; some are difficult to distinguish from B. cristatella. Their care in captivity, should they become available, will be as for B. cristatella.

Common Garden Lizard

Calotes versicolor has a wide range, from Iran and Pakistan, through India and Sri Lanka, Thailand, southern China and Sumatra. It measures up to 150mm SVL, 400mm TL. Juveniles and females are basically pale brown or buff, but with darker tails. Males in breeding condition are particularly colourful, with red throats (hence one of their common names of Bloodsucker Lizard) and extensive red coloration on their bodies. Their heads may be bright yellow or green, depending on their origin. In males, a dorsal crest of elongated, backward-pointing scales goes from the nape of the neck to the base of the tail, but females only have crests on their necks. Even in the same individual, colours can change dramatically according to temperature and mood. Excited males are among the most colourful vivarium lizards.

Availability

C. versicolor is occasionally imported but not bred in captivity to any great extent, regrettably.

Life in the wild

These lizards occupy open places at the fringes of forests and in clearings. They are commonly seen on the trunks of trees lining the roads and they also live on rocks and even garden walls. In built-up areas and tourist locations they become habituated to human activities and will even display to humans by nodding their heads.

Care in captivity

This species requires similar care to that of most other tropical dragon lizards, but it adapts to captivity much better than most of the others.

Housing Provide a large, tall, vivarium with plenty of dead branches on which the lizards can climb, and a substrate of bark chippings, leaf litter or potting compost. Spray the enclosure on a daily basis – preferably once in the morning and again in the evening – but do not allow the air to become stagnant. Good ventilation is essential.

A background temperature of 25-30°C during the day suits the lizards and there should be a basking area providing a hot-spot of 35-40°C. The temperature throughout the enclosure can be allowed to drop to 20-25°C or even less at night.

Feeding The lizards eat a wide variety of food, including all the usual insect prey, as well as eggs, smaller lizards (beware!) and small mammals. They will drink droplets of water, but also drink from a water bowl if necessary.

Right: A female Common Garden Lizard, or Bloodsucker (C. versicolor) in a typical pose, clinging to a vertical tree-trunk. Enclosures for this species should be high enough to allow it to climb.

Breeding has been achieved on several occasions, mainly in Germany. Courtship and mating are stimulated by raising the humidity through more frequent spraying. Males display by head-bobbing and vigorously chase the females. Six to 14 eggs are laid in a hole that the female digs in the compost. This should be at least 10cm deep and moist. The eggs hatch in six to seven weeks at a temperature of 25-28°C and the young grow quickly on a diet of small insects. They can be reared as a group if they have plenty of places to perch and hide. Two or three potted plants, such as weeping fig *(Ficus benjamina)* placed in their enclosure will provide them with these opportunities. They can reach sexual maturity in less than one year.

Right: This juvenile Common Garden Lizard, photographed in Sri Lanka, is just beginning to show signs of the reddish coloration on its throat that gives the species its alternative name of 'Bloodsucker Lizard'.

Similar species

Calotes *is a large genus of dragon lizards with many attractive members. Their care is likely to be similar to that described for* C. versicolor, *but other species are hard to obtain. Many come from countries such as Sri Lanka, where the collection and exportation of reptiles is prohibited.*

Flying Lizard

The flying lizards (Draco species) are unmistakable. There are about 40 species altogether and, although they vary slightly in size and coloration, a general description will suffice, especially as even experts have trouble in distinguishing one species from another. They measure 80mm SVL, 200mm TL.

All species have elongated ribs which, when erected, support a large semi-circular flap of skin on each side. This flap allows them to glide from one tree to another. When not in use, the ribs and flaps are folded back against the lizard's body and look like a closely fitting cloak.

Males have a coloured throat flap, which they use to display to one another, and which varies according to species. Females also have throat flaps, but these are smaller and less brightly coloured. The dorsal coloration is brown, grey or greenish, with indistinct darker markings.

Availability

Flying lizards are rarely available.

Life in the wild

Draco species occur in Southeast Asia and the Philippines, and are restricted to rainforests with tall trees and little growth between the canopy and the ground.

These are highly arboreal lizards that live many metres above the ground on smooth tree trunks, easily crossing from one to another by gliding.

They land slightly lower than the height at which they take off but always pointing upwards, so that they gain the height lost by running up the trunk. Females come down to the forest floor to lay their eggs in nests that they dig in leaf-litter.

Care in captivity

Almost nothing is known about the care of Draco species. They are only suitable for experienced keepers and zoos. The few animals that are imported do not usually live for very long. They obviously require very tall, large enclosures, conditions that are only realistically possible in zoological gardens. Their natural diet is ants and a suitable substitute has not been found.

Right: A Flying Lizard (Draco species) in the wild. These interesting lizards are highly specialised and their care in captivity is beyond the scope of most private collectors.

Bell's Forest Dragon

The *Gonocephalus* species are also known as angle-headed lizards. *G. bellii* occurs from southern Thailand to Borneo. It is an impressive lizard, measuring 130mm SVL, 400mm TL. The dorsal crest, composed of a single row of very long spines and, at their base, a row of shorter spines on each side, gives support to the main crest. The head is roughly triangular in shape, with a throat flap that is often black in males. The body is brown or olive in colour, paler on the underside, with a pattern of pale spots and reticulations. The tail is banded in black and pale green. Juveniles and females are duller than adult males and have shorter crests.

Availability

G. bellii is rarely available, as exports from most of their countries of origin are banned.

Life in the wild

Forest dragons live on tree trunks and hanging vines, heads pointing up, and remain motionless in the hope that they will not be noticed. If they are disturbed they invariably run up the tree until they are out of reach of most terrestrial predators. Little is known about their natural history as they are difficult to observe.

Care in captivity

The animals apparently settle down well in captivity and are less easily stressed than many of the other arboreal dragon lizards. Their requirements are poorly known, but the information given for the Prickle-nape lizards (*Acanthosaura* species) would be a good starting point, although most *Gonocephalus* are larger.

Females lay small clutches of three to five eggs, which hatch after several months. Hatchlings eat well and grow quickly.

Left: *Bell's Forest Dragon* (Gonocephalus bellii) *is a large and showy forest dragon that is rarely seen in the pet trade. This male, with a partially expanded throat flap, is an especially colourful example.*

Similar species

The Chameleon Forest Dragon (Gonocephalus chamaeleontinus) comes from peninsular Malaysia and Indonesia. This is a spectacular lizard, overall green or bluish green in colour with yellow spots, and a high crest on the nape of its neck. It is unlikely to be imported as it is protected over most of its range. The Borneo Forest Dragon (G. borneensis) is similar to Bell's Forest Dragon but, again, is rarely seen in captivity. Its requirements are assumed to be similar to those of the prickle-nape lizards.

Large Forest Dragon

Measuring 150mm SVL, 560mm TL, *Gonocephalus grandis* is the largest species in the genus. The sizes given are for males; females are slightly smaller. Males also have a larger dorsal crest than females. This consists of a group of elongated needlelike scales on the neck, and a further series of elongated scales on the back, with a short but noticeable gap between the two crests. The neck crest is supported by several rows of shorter scales on either side. The main body colour is brown, greenish brown or olive, and the crests are bluish with yellow scales at the base. Females' colours are not as dark as those of males.

Availability

The Large Forest Dragon is rarely available and has only bred in captivity on a few occasions.

Similar species

Altogether there are 17 species in the genus, some rare and poorly known. They are unlikely to become available to the pet trade. Boyd's Forest Dragon (Hypsilurus boydii) *and the Southern Forest Dragon* (H. spinipes) *are both from the rainforests of eastern Australia and closely related to the* Gonocephalus *species.*

Life in the wild

This species has a wide range, from southern Thailand, through the Malaysian Peninsula and into several Indonesia islands. Like other forest dragons, it rests on tree trunks with its head pointed up, but descends to the ground occasionally. It is most commonly seen near rivers and will dive into the water if discovered in the open.

Care in captivity

Keeping this species is a challenge. The greatest difficulty with a species of this size is providing a large enough enclosure, which would need to be a room-sized, walk-in structure, with vertical branches and trunks to provide resting places for the lizards. Because these are nervous animals, they require plenty of cover and this is best provided in the form of naturally growing, bushy plants, preferably contained in pots so that they can be easily moved.

The animals need constant high humidity; an automatic misting system is the only practical way of providing this.

Feeding *G. grandis* will eat all the usual insect foods, such as crickets and locusts, waxworms, and even small rodents.

Breeding has been achieved on rare occasions. The females lay three to six eggs in a nest that they excavate in moist soil. From what little information is available, the eggs do better at low temperatures, around 20°C, hatching in 80 to 90 days. Rearing the young is not without its problems and some refuse to eat. However, healthy hatchlings feed well and grow quickly. Captive-raised young adapt well to captivity and are calmer than wild-caught animals.

Below: As its name suggests, the Large Forest Dragon is the largest species in the genus. Males are larger than females and can be very colourful, but this species is difficult to obtain and needs a very large, heavily planted enclosure.

Sailfin Lizard

Hydrosaurus amboinensis is a large and spectacular lizard, growing to one metre in total length and therefore the largest agamid lizard in the world. It lives on several of the larger islands of the Pacific region, including those of the Celebes and the Moluccas. The characteristic that gives the animals their name is the high crest, or 'sailfin', on the tail, which can be 7cm or more in height. It consists of a flap of leathery skin. Additional crests are present on the neck

Below: The Sailfin Lizard (Hydrosaurus amboinensis) *is an impressive species from the larger islands of Southeast Asia. The high crest on its tail is a characteristic shared only with the Philippine Sailfin Lizard* (H. pustulatus).

and back, but these are lower and comblike, and are higher in males than in females. Both sexes are dark green or greenish brown in colour, but mature males can develop extensive dark blue or black markings around their chins and chests.

Availability

This species is rarely available, as imports from the countries of origin are not allowed, but a few are produced on a fairly regular basis by dedicated breeders.

Life in the wild

Sailfin lizards live in trees near rivers and are strong swimmers, using the tailfin to provide additional thrust. Small individuals can also run across the water surface for short distances, paralleling the American Plumed Basilisk (*Basiliscus plumifrons*), which they resemble superficially. The toes on their hind feet are flattened and have flanges around their rims, adding to their surface area and aiding in running and swimming. Males also use the fin for display and, possibly, in thermoregulation. It is full of small blood vessels that collect the sun's heat and shunt it around the lizard's body quickly.

Care in captivity

This species is only suitable for zoological gardens and large private collections.

Housing The animals require huge enclosures with at least half the floor area given over to water deep enough for them to swim and dive into. Fit the land area with substantial branches, some of which need to overhang the water area. The lizards require a temperature of 25-28°C during the day and slightly cooler conditions at night. A hot-spot of 40-45°C and a powerful source of UV-B are also essential.

Feeding Sailfin lizards are omnivorous and will eat large insects such as locusts, fish and day-old chicks, but will also accept vegetation, including various fruits and vegetables. Variation is important. Artificial diets, such as iguana or tortoise pellets, or minced beef and egg, with added vitamins and minerals, have also been used to good effect.

Breeding has only been achieved on a few occasions. Females lay three to nine eggs, which hatch in about 100 days at an incubation temperature of 28°C. The young can be reared without too much trouble.

Philippine Sailfin Lizard

At a total length of up to 1m, *Hydrosaurus pustulatus* is similar to the larger Sailfin Lizard, but on average, the 'fin' is slightly shorter, stopping about half way down the tail, although this can vary from one animal to another and, in some mature males, the fin can be very tall – up to 8cm. This species also has a crest starting behind the head and running the length of the back, larger and more prominent in males than in females. The animals are usually dark green or greyish green in colour, paler below.

Availability

Protected in the Philippines. Obtaining captive-bred young is difficult but not impossible.

Life in the wild

The remarks about the Sailfin Lizard's ability to run across the surface of water apply equally to this species. The Philippine Sailfin Lizard is widely eaten in its country of origin, where it is

> ### Similar species
>
> Hydrosaurus weberi *is described from Indonesia. It is reported to be slightly smaller than either of the other two species, but details are hard to obtain. Some authorities do not recognise it as a true species.*

regarded as a delicacy. Due partly to this, and to the extensive deforestation in that part of the world, sailfin lizards have become increasingly rare in the Philippines.

Care in captivity

H. pustulatus requires the same care as the slightly larger *H. amboinensis*. In captivity, *H. pustulatus* seems to settle down better than its larger relative, but plenty of cover is still essential. They are highly territorial and only male

can be kept in an enclosure. Females can also be territorial. If necessary, a subordinate individual may need to be moved to a separate enclosure to prevent serious injury. Due to the lizards' natural inclination to run rapidly if threatened, both species often suffer from abraded snouts, caused by colliding with obstacles and the sides of their enclosures when they are confined. These wounds usually heal in time if treated with a topical antibiotic powder, and the skin and scales will grow back.

Temperatures and diet are as described for *Hydrosaurus amboinensis*.

Breeding Females lay several clutches of 4-10 eggs each year, burying them in damp substrate. These hatch after about 90 days at 28°C. The young grow quickly and can quadruple in weight in two months. Provide vitamin and mineral supplements for growing juveniles.

Below: This adult male Philippine Sailfin Lizard is relishing time in the garden. He is 14 years old and just over 1m long (TL). Indoors he is kept with one female in an enclosure 1.8m long, 1.8m high and 1.2m wide. His varied diet includes bearded dragon pellets, vegetables, fruits and edible flowers.

Hump-nosed, or Lyre-headed, Lizard

Lyriocephalus scutatus is a large (up to 170mm SVL, 340mm TL), spectacular and unmistakable lizard. It is deep-bodied and predominantly green, with a short dorsal crest and a prominent knob on the tip of its snout. This is larger in males than in females. Males also have a large yellow dewlap.

Availability

L. scutatus is not available at present because the only country where it occurs, Sri Lanka, has banned exports of wildlife for many years.

Life in the wild

L. scutatus lives in the montane forests of Sri Lanka, where it habitually rests head-up on vertical tree trunks.

Care in captivity

It appears that this species is not difficult to keep. It would require a tall enclosure with vertical branches and a moisture-retaining substrate, such as orchid bark or leaf-litter, as for other forest dragons. Living, large-leaved plants would provide some security for the lizards.

Temperatures in its natural habitat are moderate, ranging from 18-23°C, but occasionally reaching 28°C. A basking spot that is exposed to UV-B is essential. Daily spraying is necessary and the humidity should not drop below 65%.

Feeding This species eats insects and is reported to be especially fond of earthworms.

Breeding has been achieved in the past. Females lay three to nine eggs, which hatch after 100 to 140 days at 25-28°C. Rearing the young has proved to be very difficult and most die of nutritional problems. Note, however, that these breeding results are from at least twenty years ago. Current knowledge of nutritional requirements and, in particular, the need to provide UV-B and the means with which to do this, may increase the chances of success if these lizards ever became available once more.

Right: The Hump-nosed Lizard (Lyriocephalus scutatus) is endemic to the island of Sri Lanka. It is the only member of its genus and its bulbous nose makes it unmistakable. It is protected in its country of origin.

Similar species

There are no similar species. Sri Lanka has an interesting selection of agamids, both large and small, including several endemic Calotes species, and the rare and unusual leafnosed lizards (Ceratophora species), but they are not freely available.

Thai, or Chinese, Water Dragon

The Thai water dragon is among the most popular of the larger lizards and is widely kept and bred in captivity. Males have a total length of 900mm, of which almost two-thirds is accounted for by their tail, but females are significantly smaller, growing to 600mm in total. In both sexes the body is slightly flattened from side to side and quite stout. There is a dorsal crest of pointed scales running from the nape of the neck, down the back and onto the tail. Males have higher crests, especially on the neck. Both sexes are green in colour and have inconspicuous diagonal stripes of turquoise on their flanks. The throat and lips may be white, orange or yellow, and are brighter in males, which inflate their throat when displaying.

Availability

Thai water dragons are widely available as wild-caught adults and captive-bred young. The latter are much easier to look after and should be chosen whenever possible. Young water

dragons are sometimes imported from reptile 'farms' under the guise of captive-bred animals. These specimens often harbour internal and external parasites and should be given appropriate prophylactic drugs. Wherever possible, it is preferable to buy juveniles from a local breeder. In any case, read the advice on page 33, which should give you a good idea of how to identify healthy animals.

Right: The Thai Water Dragon is one of the most popular forest dragons. It adapts well to captivity and breeds easily, ensuring a constant supply of captive-bred juveniles.

Life in the wild

As their common name suggests, these lizards live along the margins of rivers and streams, from India to Thailand and southern China. They are arboreal and spend most of the time in branches that overhang the water, into which they will drop if they feel threatened.

Care in captivity

Given the right conditions, water dragons make spectacular display animals, so any effort and expense made in providing them with a large and attractive enclosure will be amply rewarded.

Housing Water dragons need large enclosures with substantial amounts of water. In an enclosure measuring about one metre cubed – the minimum for a single animal – the floor should be divided so that roughly 50% is an aquatic area. This should be at least 15cm deep, preferably more, and there

should be branches arranged in such a way that they overhang this area, so that the lizard can behave naturally.

For groups of adults, enclosures should measure upwards of 2mx1mx1.5 metres high, with an aquatic area of at least one square metre. However, the lizards will quickly foul the water, so there must be a convenient means of changing it, ideally a waste outlet opened by means of a tap below the enclosure. Using a small pump to circulate the water over a pile of rocks and back into the aquatic area will help to raise the humidity in the enclosure and will add interest to the set-up.

Artificial plants can be used to provide the lizards with cover. Alternatively, incorporate large, tough, living plants, such as the Swiss cheese plant (Monstera deliciosa), figs (Ficus species) or any of the many Philodendron species. All of these are climbing species and will grow up among dead branches to create a natural appearance.

The background temperature of the enclosure should be about 25-30°C and there should be some variation, with the floor of the enclosure being cooler than the top. Install a basking light to create a hot-spot of 35-40°C. A source of UV-B is also necessary but, since you are dealing with a forest species, this does not need to be as intense as for desert lizards, such as, say, bearded dragons. The easiest way to achieve this is simply to use one of the low-powered UV-B tubes. In addition, a good growth of plants will allow the lizard to shelter from intense light, if this is what it prefers.

Feeding Thai water dragons readily eat all the usual livefoods, including crickets, locusts and waxworms, and will sometimes accept vegetable matter as well, although they may be reluctant to do so. Juveniles are exclusively insectivorous and will take any insect food of appropriate size. Follow the advice on pages 81-82 regarding supplements, especially for breeding females and growing young.

Above: *Thai Water Dragons typically rest with their heads raised, giving an impression of alertness. Individuals that fail to do this may be too cool or suffering from other complaints.*

Breeding is achieved regularly and some breeders produce large numbers of young water dragons each year. Animals in good condition will mate at almost any time of the year, but autumn seems to be the time when breeding activity reaches its peak. Males become more colourful at this time and display by lowering their brightly coloured dewlap and standing in front of females, blocking their path and showing off their colours and markings. At the same time, they nod their head vigorously and the females respond with a submissive arm-waving action, similar to that of bearded dragons. Young and subordinate males respond in the same way and overt aggression is usually avoided.

Mating occurs after the male has mounted the female and gripped the nape of her neck in his jaws. Egg-laying occurs one to two months later. The female will require a depth of at least 20cm of moist soil, or sand/soil mixture, in which to excavate a nest. Once she is satisfied with the position and depth of the nest she lays five to 20 eggs before replacing the substrate and smoothing over the surface to disguise its position. Unless you witness the egg-laying, the only sign is often the emaciated condition of the female immediately after she has disposed of her eggs.

Carefully remove the eggs from the nest and incubate them artificially, as described on page 99. At 25-28°C they will hatch in 50 to 60 days. Leave them in the incubator until the young are completely free of the egg and have started to move around; the security and humidity in the incubator will help them get off to a good start.

The young can be set up as a group in a smaller enclosure, including a glass tank with mesh lid, but a large water dish should also be available to them, as well as plenty of opportunities to climb and bask. Baby water dragons are among the most engaging lizards and respond to their owner once they have learned where their food comes from. They grow quickly and will need to be moved on to larger enclosures several times before they reach adult size, which takes between 12 and 18 months.

Above: Male Thai Water Dragons have more colourful lips and throats than females. In this case, the throat has a purplish tinge.

Left: Thai Water Dragons need the opportunity to enter water, which can be provided in a large bowl, as here, or as part of a divided vivarium.

Australian Water Dragon

Physignathus lesueurii can grow to 245mm SVL, 750mm TL, exceptionally to 1m. Males are significantly larger than females. This species is not as brightly coloured as the Thai Water Dragon and occurs in two distinct forms. The Eastern Water Dragon *(P. lesueurii lesueurii)* has an obvious dark stripe from its eye to its neck, black bands on the body and a large reddish area on the throat and chest, more colourful in males. The Gippsland Water Dragon, *(P. lesueurii howittii)* lacks the black stripes on the face and back and the red flush to its chest, and is brown or olive with paler stripes across its back and flanks. Both subspecies have a crest of pointed scales on the nape of their neck, extending down their back. The body and tail are flattened from side to side as an adaptation to swimming; these water dragons are highly aquatic.

Availability

The export of reptiles from Australia is forbidden, so all Australian water dragons offered for sale are captive-bred. It appears that they are all of the more colourful, eastern form *(P. l. lesueurii)*. Obtaining captive-bred stock is difficult but by no means impossible.

Care in captivity

This species is often less nervous than the Thai Water Dragon, but this may simply be because the animals are (or should be) bred in captivity. They are also more tolerant of low temperatures and can be kept in outside enclosures in some places, such as the southern United States. In Europe, outside enclosures would require

Distinguishing subspecies

This example belongs to the eastern subspecies P. lesueurii lesueurii. *It can be distinguished from the other subspecies* (P. l. howittii) *by the thick dark line behind its eye and the red flush to its throat and underside.*

The long whiplike tail of this and many other dragon lizards can be used as a weapon, but tame animals rarely do this.

Above: The Australian Water Dragon (Physignathus lesueurii lesueurii) *is bred in captivity in small numbers. It is a tough and adaptable species and makes a good alternative to the Thai Water Dragon, to which it is closely related.*

protection from frost, in a large heated greenhouse, for instance, or the lizards would need to be rehoused in the winter.

Provide young animals with heat during the winter and do not allow them to hibernate. In all other respects, the enclosure layout, heating and lighting, etc., are as for the Thai Water Dragon.

Feeding The Australian Water Dragon's diet is similar to that of the Thai Water Dragon, but there are reports that animals will eat tinned dog and cat food, as well as fruit and vegetables. They also eat fish, frogs and mice.

Breeding takes place in the spring and males develop intense red chests at this time. If more than one male is present, they should be separated to avoid fighting. Females lay up to 20 eggs in a hole that they excavate in moist soil and only rarely lay a second clutch. The eggs hatch after about 80 to 100 days and the young are 12cm long. Rearing them is straightforward as long as they are given the correct conditions – in particular, UV-B and vitamin and mineral supplements.

GROUND AND ROCK AGAMAS

Left: *A male Mwanza Flat-headed Agama* (Agama mwanzae), *photographed in Tanzania.*

Above: *A Toad-headed Agama* (Phrynocephalus arabicus). *These lizards are superbly adapted to live in desert environments.*

In many respects, the ground and rock agamas from Africa, the Middle East and Central Asia are smaller versions of the bearded dragons and require similar conditions In captivity. The key to keeping them healthy is bright conditions, plenty of heat and UV-B, but these animals also need spacious enclosures and opportunities to bask and display. This will not only allow them to thrive and encourage them to breed, but will also create conditions under which their brilliant colours, especially those of the males, will develop to their best advantage. As they become harder to obtain, captive-breeding should become more worthwhile and more information will become available. Results with a few species, especially two forms of the Starred Agama *(Laudakia stellio)* are encouraging. On the other hand, the habits and captive care of some species, notably the toad-headed agamas, are virtually unknown, and this may be an area in which experienced and committed hobbyists could make an important contribution.

Red-headed Agama

Agama agama is a conspicuous and distinctive lizard from East Africa, measuring 120-180mm SVL, 200-300mm TL. Breeding males have bright blue bodies and a red or orange head. Subordinate males lack these bright colours and are duller like the females, which are grey with darker markings on their backs.

Availability

These lizards are sometimes available, but never as captive-bred stock. Wild individuals may harbour parasites and appropriate precautions need to be taken.

Life in the wild

Males can often be seen displaying and basking on the most prominent rocks. *Agama agama* also lives around human habitations, where it uses brickwork and thatched roofs. Colonies consist of a dominant male, several younger or subordinate males and a number of females. Males that begin to colour up are seen as a direct challenge to the dominant male who will display to them by bobbing his head and doing push-ups. If this fails, the subordinate male is chased out of the territory.

Care in captivity

These beautiful lizards need similar conditions to bearded dragons: a bright, dry and warm enclosure with a powerful spotlight producing heat and bright light, and a good source of UV-B. Temperatures below the spotlight should reach 40°C minimum during the day, with a substantial drop in temperature – to about 15-20°C – at night. The substrate should be sand or gravel with piles of rocks for basking or displaying and retreats for hiding.

Feeding The lizards are insectivores and will eat crickets and locusts, although a wider variety of food is preferable, especially if you hope to breed them. They sometimes take a small amount of plant material, especially flowers. Provide vitamin and calcium supplements. The animals will drink from a bowl but will also lick drops of water from the sides of their enclosure if these are lightly sprayed every day.

Right: A male Red-headed Agama (Agama agama), photographed in Tanzania 'warming up' on roof tiles. Dominant males of this species have spectacular coloration, but females and subordinate males are more sombre.

Similar species

The Mwanza Flat-headed Agama (Agama mwanzae) is also East African, but almost completely restricted to Tanzania. It is similar to the red-headed agama but is, if anything, even more brightly coloured, as its head and the upper part of its back are brilliant pink. It is rarely if ever available but, if it were to be, its care would be similar to that of the red-headed agama.

Breeding It is not possible to keep more than one male in the same enclosure, but a colony of one male and up to three females is perfectly possible. Breeding activity, in the form of head-bobbing and chasing, may result once the lizards have settled in. Females lay up to 12 eggs, which they bury in sand or soil. They should be removed from the enclosure and incubated at 28°C, when they will hatch after about 50-60 days.

Left: A male Mwanza Flat-headed Agama (Agama mwanzae). These agamas are almost unbelievably colourful. This dominant male is posing on a small rock in Central Tanzania. The species is not widely available at present.

Southern Rock Agama

Although *Agama atra* is slightly smaller than the Red-headed Agama (70-120mm SVL, 100-188mm TL) and has a flattened body, this species is typical of the members of its genus. Males are larger than females and more brightly coloured, being brown or greenish with an electric blue head and a white stripe down the centre of their back. Their undersides, which they display when doing 'push-ups' are bright blue. Females are grey with darker markings and develop orange or red spots on their flanks when they are gravid.

Like other agamas, males are highly territorial and will not tolerate other brightly coloured males.

Similar species

The Namibian Rock Agama (Agama planiceps) is similar in shape and lifestyle, but dominant males have bright red heads and tails and deep blue bodies. Females are brown with a number of lemon-yellow streaks on their heads and a bright orange marking on their flanks. Its care in captivity is assumed to be similar to that of the other Agama species. The Southern Spiny Agama (Agama hispida) is also from South Africa, but lives on the ground among shrubs and bushes. It hides in burrows at the bases of bushes. Nothing is known about its care in captivity.

Availability

Agama atra is rarely available and not bred in captivity as far as is known.

Life in the wild

Agama atra is confined to South Africa and southern Namibia, where it inhabits rock outcrops and mountains.

Care in captivity

Agama atra requires the same care as the Red-headed Agama. However, it is not associated with humans and usually lives on rock outcrops, so bear this in mind when setting up an enclosure. In addition, *A. atra* has a more southerly distribution and probably requires a cool period to simulate its natural winter if it is to breed in captivity, although this needs to be confirmed.

Right: The Southern Rock Agama (Agama atra) is the most common species in rocky parts of South Africa. The male (shown here) has a bright blue head and a white line down its back. It is frequently seen head-bobbing on prominent rocky outcrops.

Starred Agama, or Hardun

The Starred Agama is a thick-set lizard with a broad, flattened body and triangular head. It measures up to about 200mm SVL, 300mm TL. Random enlarged scales are scattered over its skin, especially on the flanks, and its tail has rings of pointed, spiny scales.

Five subspecies are recognised. Colours vary somewhat between subspecies but there is also variation within subspecies, making it difficult to identify individuals to this level unless their origin is known. Individuals can also vary according to their temperature and mood.

Eastern European specimens are usually light to dark brown, with a row of large yellowish or tan blotches down their backs. The tail often has alternating light and dark rings. One of the most distinctive subspecies is *L. s. picea* from the Middle East, a small form, growing to about 200mm total length and attractively marked with orange spots on a black background. It is endemic to lava fields of the Middle East, where its black and orange markings make it difficult to see when it is in its natural habitat of black volcanic rock with scattered blotches of orange lichen. Males are less heavily marked with spots

Right: *The Starred Agama* (Laudakia stellio) *is the only agamid to occur in Europe, and lives on several Greek Islands. The European subspecies, seen here on Lesbos, is* L. stellio stellio. *Other subspecies occur in the Middle East.*

than females and develop a dark blue throat in the breeding season.

Another form, the Painted Agama *(Laudakia stellio brachydactyla)*, from Israel and the Arabian Peninsula, is also kept and bred successfully. This is a slightly larger subspecies that becomes especially tame, learning to take food from its owner's fingers. It is pale brown or sandy brown in colour, with extensive yellow or tan markings on its body, legs and tail.

Availability

The Starred Agama is rarely if ever imported, but the orange-spotted and painted forms described above are bred in captivity on a small scale.

Life in the wild

This is the only agama native to Europe, where it is found on several Greek islands. Its range extends through the Middle East and into northern Egypt. These species are often seen on the dry stone walls common in the parts of the world where they live.

Care in captivity

The following notes apply mostly to the orange-spotted form *L. s. picea* and the Painted Agama *(L. s. brachydactyla)*, although the care and breeding of all the forms is likely to be similar.

Housing These active, heat-loving lizards require similar conditions to the *Agama* species, although they are not as nervous and less inclined to dash madly around the enclosure if disturbed. Even so, a large terrarium, at least one metre long, is recommended. It should have a sandy substrate and stable piles of rocks for the lizards to climb and bask on. You could replicate in miniature the dry stone walls found in their natural habitat. Plants are unnecessary and, in any case, would probably not survive in an enclosure with these lizards.

Create a hot-spot at one end of the enclosure, with a temperature of at least 40°C. The other end should be cooler, with places for the lizards to shelter. The temperature can be allowed to drop to room temperature at night, and daytime temperatures should be reduced by 5-10°C in the winter if you hope to breed the lizards. They require large doses of UV-B and should be able to bask very close to the source. A calcium and mineral supplement is also essential, especially for breeding females and growing young.

Feeding These lizards consume all the usual insect foods, such as locusts and crickets. They also eat leaves of salad and other plants such as dandelions and cresses. Offer these regularly.

Breeding occurs in response to rising temperature and increasing daylength in the spring. Males become highly territorial at this time. Only keep one male per enclosure, although a single male can be housed with two or more females in a harem arrangement. Females lay clutches of six to 12 eggs and will produce several clutches in the course of a single breeding season, laying at intervals of about five to six weeks provided they are fed well.

When the female begins to swell with eggs, provide an area of damp substrate or a special laying box containing damp peat/sand mixture. The eggs hatch in 50 to 60 days at a temperature of 28-30°C and the young are relatively small at about 2.5-3cm. They usually feed well on small insects and grow quickly, reaching sexual maturity in one or two years.

Below: *The Starred Agama is a rock-dweller, often seen on dry stone walls and ancient ruins, basking and displaying. It is one of the more robust and easily kept species.*

Similar species

There are an additional 20 species in the genus Laudakia *but, as far as is known, none of them is available through the normal channels. Recently, a small agama from the Middle East,* Pseudotrapelus sinaitus, *previously known as* Agama sinaita, *has been imported into Europe. Being smaller than most other agamas, this species may adapt to captivity better than some of the others. High temperatures and plenty of UV-B are indicated.*

Toad-headed agamas

There are 41 species of *Phrynocephalus* recognised at present, although there is some disagreement among experts as to their relationships with each other. They occur in the arid parts of the Middle East, Central Asia and the Arabian Peninsula. They are moderate in size, ranging from 120-250mm in total length, and have broad, flattened bodies, narrow necks and proportionately large heads.

Availability

These agamas are rarely available. Reports of animals in captivity tend to result from specimens collected by the keeper, an activity

that is increasingly difficult nowadays due to the protection of wildlife in many regions and the unstable political situation in many of the countries in which they live.

Life in the wild

Some species, notably *Phrynocephalus mystaceus*, with a wide distribution in Central Asia, have brightly coloured patches of skin

that are normally hidden, on their throat or in the groin region, for instance, and they use these to display to each other. However, most rely on camouflage and are grey, yellowish or

Below: Toad-headed agamas, such as Phrynocephalus arabicus, *are interesting small agamids from the deserts of Central Asia and the Middle East but they are rarely seen in captivity.*

tan in colour, depending on the substrate on which they live, and have speckled and random markings that break up their outline. Many are almost impossible to see when they remain motionless and, in this respect, they closely parallel other lizards, such as the American Horned Lizards (*Phrynosoma* species).

On the other hand, species that live among sand dunes, such as the Arabian Toad-headed Agama (*P. arabicus*) shuffle down into the sand by flattening their bodies and moving rapidly from side to side until they disappear beneath the surface.

The toad-headed agama uses its tail for balance when it is running quickly, raising it off the ground, and also uses it for display. Some species have coloured tips to their tails, which they coil and uncoil like a watch-spring to attract attention. They are sit-and-wait predators, remaining motionless while raising their bodies off the ground on straightened legs, or perching on a rock or in low vegetation until an insect comes within range.

Care in captivity

Little is known, but a careful study of the agamas' natural behaviour will help to arrive at a suitable set-up.

Housing Conditions should be dry, with a substrate of sand or gravel, depending on species, but there should be a damp area beneath a rock or an artificial hide. Captive

animals have been known to drown in even small water bowls, which are unnecessary if the cool end of the enclosure is lightly sprayed occasionally. These agamas are capable of absorbing water from the substrate. The water tracks up by capillary action through small channels in their skin, eventually leading to the corners of the mouth. (An Australian agamid, *Moloch horridus*, has similar behaviour.)

Decorate the enclosure with rocks and driftwood, which will give the lizards opportunities to perch and bask. UV-B in high doses is essential. The animals require very high temperatures, but with an opportunity to move away from the heat to a cooler part of the enclosure if necessary. Night-time temperatures can be allowed to fall, but this will depend on the species: those from high altitudes in Central Asia, for example, are probably capable of surviving temperature drops to near zero, whereas those from the deserts of Arabia could be expected to be far less tolerant. It is impossible to be precise, and some research on their places of origin will be necessary.

Feeding All species are insectivorous and probably eat mostly ants in the wild, but will take crickets, waxworms and flies in captivity. Occasional meals of ants may be essential to keep them in good health.

Breeding has not been achieved in captivity. Wild-caught females have laid clutches of two to ten eggs *(P. helioscopus)*, which hatched after 30 to 40 days. The young measured 23-28mm in length, but grew quickly, reaching adult size in less than one year.

Toad-headed lizards are thought to be short-lived even in the wild, and captives have rarely survived more than a few months. Using recently developed techniques and equipment, it may be possible to keep and breed them in captivity with greater success if stock could be obtained.

Below: Toad-headed lizards get their common and scientific names from their flattened heads. All species are highly adapted to living in open deserts, where they are well camouflaged and feed on small invertebrates such as ants.

DAB LIZARDS AND BUTTERFLY AGAMAS

Left: An Ornate Dab Lizard (Uromastyx ornata), *on the lookout near its rocky burrow.*

Above: *Reeve's Butterfly Agama* (Leiolepis reevesii) *lives in Southeast Asia and southern China.*

Uromastyx species are variously known as mastigures, dab lizards, dhub lizards and spiny-tailed lizards. Of the 17 or 18 species, about half are available from time to time, either through the pet trade or from private breeders. Dab lizards are interesting agamids, usually assigned to a separate subfamily, the Leiolepinae, along with the butterfly agamas. Wherever possible, you should obtain captive-bred animals, as these adapt much more easily to captivity and do not present their owner with the stress, and possible financial loss, that wild ones often do. Furthermore, it is likely that the collection and export of dab lizards from Egypt and other countries will be stopped in the near future as populations are suffering from over-collection. All dab lizards have been placed on Appendix 2 of CITES, which monitors and limits trade in them. Buying directly from the breeder has many advantages, as the breeder should be willing to provide advice on caring for your new animals and may offer an 'after-sales' service if you run into problems later on.

Dab Lizards

Dab lizards occur over a wide region, from North Africa, through the Middle East to northwest India, and are restricted to arid habitats. Although there is some variation between the species, they tend to live in colonies of around 20 individuals, excavating a network of burrows in rocky slopes away from sand dunes and preferably in areas where there are bushy plants to provide food and cover. The burrows can be over 3m long, with a main chamber over 1m below the surface. The colony lives and feeds in the vicinity of the burrows, but at the height of summer it may have to travel over 1km to find food, which may consist of a dried-up bush. In the spring, when there is fresh plant growth, the animals select flower buds, leaves and fresh twigs to eat and feed heavily, replacing any weight they lost during the winter. They are especially fond of yellow flowers.

Most species hibernate in winter and do not

Below: An Ornate Dab Lizard (Uromastyx ornata) just outside the entrance to its burrow. The yellow and blue coloration is very well defined here.

Obtaining stock

Unfortunately, captive-bred animals are not always easy to locate. Joining a herpetological society gives you access to private advertisements through its newsletters. Reptile shows (expositions) are also good places to find stock; some of them insist that all animals offered for sale are captive-bred. Buying directly from the breeder has many advantages, as the breeder should be willing to provide advice on caring for your new animals and may offer an 'after-sales' service if you run into problems later on.

An alternative for those who do not live near places where meetings and shows take place is to sign-up to an internet forum, of which there are several, and monitor advertisements or even advertise for animals wanted. As young dab lizards cannot be sexed accurately, you will need to buy a small group – say four – and hope there is at least one pair among them. Keeping in touch with the breeder is a good idea because it may be possible to exchange surplus animals with others if they also end up with a poor sex ratio – hopefully one that is 'the other way round' to yours.

emerge from their burrows unless the night-time temperature reaches at least 22°C. In the day they bask until their body temperature rises above 38°C, at which point they begin to forage for food. This information is taken from studies of the North African *Uromastyx acanthinura*, but other species have similar lifestyles. From this information it should be obvious that dab lizards require spacious, dry and hot conditions.

Availability

The species that are most likely to be available captive-bred are the Spiny-tailed Dab Lizard *(U. acanthinura)* in very small numbers, the Egyptian Dab Lizard *(U. aegyptia)*, Mali Dab Lizard *(U. dispar maliensis)*, Geyr's Dab Lizard *(U. geyri)* and the Ornate Dab Lizard *(U. ornata)*, although any of the species mentioned earlier are possibilities.

Care in captivity

The *Uromastyx* species have a specialised lifestyle and their captive care needs, therefore, to be equally specialised. Problems associated with keeping dab lizards include the high density of gut parasites with which imported animals are invariably infested. Some intestinal flora is natural in plant-eating lizards – perhaps even essential. However, if the parasite load becomes overbearing due to stress, it puts the animal's health at risk. Establishing a healthy colony from wild-caught animals is not easy and involves testing for nematodes (roundworms) and protozoans, especially *Entamoeba*. *Entamoeba* causes diarrhoea, which will result in infested specimens excreting copious amounts of liquid faeces. Unless the parasites are eliminated promptly the lizards will die from dehydration. Furthermore, rehydration is not always easy as it is not in these lizards' natures to drink. Under natural conditions they obtain most of their water from their food, and protect themselves against water loss by living in deep burrows and having waterproof skin. All newly acquired, wild-caught dab lizards should be placed in a pan of shallow water for at least 10 minutes every day so that they can absorb some water.

Collect faecal samples and send them off for laboratory examination. If parasites are detected in a faecal sample, treatment with the appropriate drugs needs to go hand-in-hand with oral rehydration using water or an electrolyte solution. Seek veterinary advice, but even with early treatment, there are likely to be losses.

Housing Dab lizards, especially the larger species such as *U. acanthinura* and *U. aegyptia*, require plenty of floor space. An enclosure measuring 2x1m is suitable for a pair or trio of these species, but height is not so important. If the sides are made from a smooth material, such as glass or plastic, it may not even be necessary to cover the enclosure (unless other pets or small children are likely to climb in). Smaller species, and juveniles of the larger ones, can be housed in smaller enclosures, but a length of one metre should be regarded as a minimum.

The substrate can be sand or rounded gravel (pea gravel) unless the lizards are newly imported, in which case it should be newspaper or kitchen paper towelling. This makes it easier to check the faeces and change the substrate frequently. Some keepers use rabbit pellets or alfalfa pellets as a substrate, but these unnatural substances tend to disintegrate after a while and are probably best avoided.

Flat rocks or bricks piled up under the heat lamp provide basking places. Place additional piles of rocks, large pieces of driftwood or mangrove root, a section of terracotta drain-pipe or an artificial hide at the coolest end of the enclosure to provide some shelter. Try to avoid over-elaborate rock structures as the lizards are avid diggers and may dislodge piles of rocks, with unfortunate consequences.

Some keepers create artificial floors to their enclosures, with holes leading to the lower level, to recreate the tunnel systems that dab lizards inhabit in the wild, but this is not strictly necessary. Natural plants are unlikely to survive, due to the hot, dry conditions and the herbivorous natures of the lizards.

Feeding Young dab lizards will eat some insect food and can be offered occasional insects, such as waxworms and mealworms, but these should only make up a small proportion of their diet: about 10% at most. (Hardwick's Dab Lizard is an exception, as its natural diet appears to include more insects than the other species.)

Adult dab lizards are almost entirely herbivorous. A basic diet for all ages should include at least 50% green leaf vegetables, such as kale, cress, clover and dandelion leaves. Lettuce leaves can be offered in moderation, but they are poor in many nutrients. Dab lizards also like to eat the flowers of dandelion and other yellow-flowered plants. The remaining 50% of the diet can be made up with beans, peas, carrot (if they will eat it) and sweetcorn. Beans and peas can be given complete with the pods. The lizards will also eat hay, artificial diets formulated for iguanas and even rabbit pellets, but these drier foods should be given in small quantities, mixed in with the fresh food.

Soft fruit is not a natural food for dab lizards, but you can give them small quantities if they

Below: These Uromastyx ocellata *are similar to but more slender than* U. ornata. *The captive care of all these species is fundamentally different from that of other agama lizards and, while they can be rewarding reptiles to keep in captivity, they represent a serious undertaking.*

like it. In the wild, dab lizards eat grass and cereal seeds that blow in from neighbouring fertile areas, and some will eat bird seeds, such as millet and sunflower, in captivity. Sprouted seeds and beans are especially nutritious.

Mix calcium and multivitamin and mineral supplements with the lizards' food. Only small amounts are necessary, as long as the animals are given plenty of heat to help their digestion, have access to UV-B and are offered a wide variety of plants to eat.

Heating and lighting Heat lamps and UV-B lamps should be installed as for bearded dragons. A temperature of at least 40-50°C is necessary under the basking light. Without this they cannot digest their food efficiently and, even if they eat well, they may lose weight. These lizards cannot survive in indoor enclosures without a source of UV-B. Those keepers fortunate enough to live in hot, sunny places may be able to keep dab lizards outdoors for

part of the year. Natural sunlight has beneficial effects on the lizards, both physiologically and psychologically.

If you intend to breed dab lizards, they will need a seasonal light cycle. This should be based on a 16:8 photoperiod: in summer the lights and heaters should be left on for 16 hours and turned off for eight. In the winter the timings should be reversed, so that the light and heat is on for eight hours and off for 16. Adjusting the photoperiod by one hour at a time over a two or three month period is more natural than a sudden change.

Daytime temperatures should be reduced during the winter as well and, as long as the background heat of the room does not fall below about 15°C, heating and lighting can be turned off completely for four to six weeks in the middle of winter. This will encourage the lizards to go through a period of dormancy, which appears to be essential if they are to breed. They will stop eating altogether and may lose

Left: A gravid female Uromastyx nigriventris. *This species is found in the Atlas Mountains across Morocco and Algeria.*

significant amounts of weight but, as long as they were feeding well prior to dormancy, this should not be a cause for concern.

As the temperature and daylength increase again in the spring, the lizards will resume feeding and should be given plenty of fresh greens. Breeding activity will normally occur at this time. Animals that are thin or in poor condition should not be hibernated. Some breeders prefer to keep juveniles active during the winter so that their growth is not arrested.

Breeding Sex determination is only possible with adult dab lizards. Males have broader heads and, in most species, larger femoral pores. In the breeding season the males' pores secrete a waxlike substance that gives them a frilly appearance. Males can be aggressive towards each other and serious fighting usually indicates that the group contains more than one male. Males display to females by chasing and by performing typical agamid press-ups in front of them. Some biting takes place but injuries are rare.

If mating is successful, the female begins to swell with eggs and you must make some provision for egg laying. This can be a large wooden or plastic box filled to a good depth, at least 20cm, with a moist sand and peat mixture. Part of the box should be covered to retain moisture and to give the female some seclusion; some breeders use a plastic box with a large hole cut in the lid and this works quite well. The

eggs, which vary in size and number according to the species, should be removed to a separate container with a similar mixture and incubated at 30-32°C.

The young are easy to rear on a diet similar to that of the adults, but chopped up into smaller portions. Insects can make up a larger proportion of their food at first and vitamin and mineral supplements, especially calcium, should be added to every meal. The young grow quickly at first, but can take several years to reach sexual maturity.

Above: *A one-month-old* Uromastyx thomasi *weighing about 25gm. Note the short snout and paddle-shaped tail of this species from Oman.*

Spiny-tailed Dab Lizard

Uromastyx acanthinura is a large species – 250mm SVL, 400mm TL – with a wide, flattened body, broad head and thick tail. The tail has a series of spiny rings around it and the lizard can use this as a club and to block its tunnel against any pursuing predator, such as a snake. The lizard is highly variable in colour and may be yellowish brown, yellow, orange, red or green. Over this is a pattern of black spots, sometimes arranged into vague crossbars. In breeding animals, the sides of the head, throat and forelimbs are often jet black. Both sexes are the same colours, but older males develop broader heads, while females in good condition are often more rotund than males.

Availability

U. acanthinura is bred in small numbers by specialist breeders and consequently expensive. Wild-caught animals have not been available for several years.

Care in captivity

Being a large, bulky species, the spiny-tailed dab lizard requires a large enclosure, at least 2mx50cmx50cm for a pair or small group of adults. General care and feeding is as described on pages 183-187.

A period of inactivity, or partial hibernation, is essential with this species if you hope to breed it. Even if they are not to be bred, adults should be given a short winter cooling period, followed by increasing daylength and temperature in the spring to stimulate feeding and natural behaviour. Clutches of 12 and 14 eggs have been reported. At 30°C these hatch in about 90 to 100 days.

Below: *The Spiny-tailed Dab Lizard* (Uromastyx acanthinura) *is a large and impressive lizard that adapts well to captivity provided its specialised requirements are met.*

Similar species

Geyr's Dab Lizard (U. geyri) *is very similar to but more slender in overall body shape than* U. acanthinura. *The two species intergrade in parts of North Africa and it is not always possible to separate them. To all intents and purposes they can be cared for in the same way. Other African species – the Sudan Dab Lizard* (U. dispar) *and the Mali Dab Lizard* (U. dispar maliensis) *– are of similar size though rarely as colourful as* U. acanthinura. *These are sometimes listed, but often the true identity of individuals is questionable. Care and breeding are assumed to be similar.*

Above: *The Saharan, or Geyr's, Dab Lizard* (Uromastyx geyri) *is closely related to the Spiny-tailed Dab Lizard, but this specimen shows the more slender body shape, different coloration and less spiny tail.*

Right: *The underside of Geyr's Dab Lizard has a bold patterning in yellow and brown, an effective camouflage in its native arid environment.*

The tail is impressively sturdy but not quite as spiny as that of U. acanthinura.

Egyptian Dab Lizard

Growing to 750mm, *Uromastyx aegyptia* is the largest member of the genus and is usually easy to recognise due to its uniform brown or yellowish coloration and small scales. It has a heavily spined, club-shaped tail that it can use as a weapon. Juveniles are more distinctly marked, with rows of pale grey or white spots crossing their backs. As they grow, the spots become further apart and darken until, in adults, they are barely visible. The species is found throughout Egypt and neighbouring countries. A separate

Below: An Egyptian Dab Lizard surveying its surroundings in the heat of the day. The gravel slope here is a typical habitat for these desert lizards. Note the small scales of its skin.

subspecies, *U. a. microlepis*, occurs in the southeast of the Arabian Peninsula, where it is known as the 'dhub'. It lives in deserts, especially on gravel plains, where it digs extensive burrows.

Availability

This species has been imported in large numbers but not in recent years. Captive breeding has been achieved but captive-bred young are not generally available.

Care in captivity

See pages 183-187 for general care advice. Breeding takes place in the spring after a period of winter dormancy and females lay 10 to 40 eggs. These take about 100 days to hatch and the young are easy to rear, but take three to four years to reach sexual maturity. In contrast to most other dab lizards, this species can be very shy in captivity, retreating into a hide box at the slightest disturbance.

Similar species

Leptien's Dab Lizard (U. leptieni) *from the United Arab Emirates and parts of Oman, is sometimes recognised as a separate species but is probably a subspecies of* U. aegyptia. *It is not available through the pet trade.*

Below: *This Leptien's Dab Lizard* (U. aegyptia leptieni) *from the Arabian Peninsula, illustrates the tortoise-like head and heavy body of this species.*

Hardwick's Dab Lizard

Even these subtle markings will fade with maturity.

Uromastyx hardwickii is a medium-sized dab lizard, growing to 400-500mm. Females are slightly smaller than males. The lizards are yellowish-brown in colour without distinct markings, just a mottled pattern of dark and light patches over their backs. They are easily distinguished from other dab lizards by their tail, which lacks the large spines that give the genus one of its common names (spiny-tailed lizards). Instead, they have rings of smaller spines, little more than pointed conical knobs. Their heads are more rounded than those of the other species and their snouts are even blunter and more tortoiselike.

Hardwick's Dab Lizard comes from Pakistan, India and Afghanistan. In 2009 an older generic name of *Saara* was resurrected for this species, together with two others, *U. asmussi* and *U. loricata*, but this has not been widely accepted at the time of writing.

Availability

Hardwick's Dab Lizard is imported occasionally, but rarely if ever bred in captivity. Imported animals are often juveniles, giving the false impression that this is a 'dwarf' species.

Above: *This juvenile Hardwick's Dab Lizard shows the typical blunt head, indistinct patterning and less spiny tail.*

Care in captivity

Care is as for other dab lizards but, being slightly smaller, *U. hardwickii* can be housed in a smaller enclosure. It is a very docile species that soon becomes tame.

Right: *An adult Hardwick's Dab Lizard at home in its enclosure, complete with a hideaway. This species has a dull adult coloration compared to some other more striking species of* Uromastyx.

Similar species

U. asmussi *and* U. loricata *occur in the same general area as* U. hardwickii, *extending into Iraq and Iran. They are never available through the pet trade and unlikely to be in the foreseeable future owing to the political situation in their countries of origin. Apart from these two rare dab lizards, Hardwick's Dab Lizard is distinct from other members of the genus.*

Ornate Dab Lizard

At just over 300mm for males and just under 300mm for females, *Uromastyx ornata* is the smallest of the commonly available dab lizards. It is also arguably the most colourful, being blue-grey, blue or greenish yellow, with bright yellow markings arranged as rows of spots across its back. The coloration on the flanks and sides of the head is usually a more intense blue than that on the upper surface, and the lizards also have yellow markings on the head. Males are noticeably brighter than females, some of which have pale yellow markings on a brown or tan background. However, there is great variability between individuals (of both sexes) and even in the same individual, depending on temperature and general condition.

This is the easiest of the *Uromastyx* species to sex. For confirmation, examine the femoral pores, which are significantly larger in males and often have conspicuous frills resulting from the waxy substance they secrete. Males also have larger heads and more powerful jaws.

Availability

At the time of writing, *U. ornata* is the most readily available species of *Uromastyx*. Wild-caught animals are being imported in quite large numbers and many breeders are having limited success with this species. The advice on acclimatising dab lizards (page 183) is especially relevant to this species and it is important to

Similar species

The Eyed Dab Lizard (U. ocellata) *is very similar but slightly less colourful. However, the two species were formerly regarded as one (with* U. ornata *as a subspecies of* U. ocellata*) and there is some confusion over the identities of older descriptions and photographs.* Uromastyx ocellata, *as currently understood, comes from southern Egypt and neighbouring countries.* Uromastyx benti *is from Yemen and* U. macfadyeni *is from Somalia, but these have never been available. One other 'species' from the region,* U. philbyi, *is regarded as a subspecies of* U. ornata.

select healthy individuals. Wherever possible, choose captive-bred animals, even if they are more expensive.

Life in the wild

Ornate Dab Lizards occur in Egypt, Israel and the Arabian Peninsula. They live in colonies, in rocky deserts and wadis (dry riverbeds).

Care in captivity

This should be as described on pages 183-187. The Ornate Dab Lizard is one of the calmer species and makes a good display animal, as long as it is healthy and kept in the correct conditions. Individuals soon become tame and will approach their owner for food.

Below: Looking closely at the head reveals an intricate patterning of scales. These are attractive lizards that become familiar and fascinating pet animals.

Above: The Ornate Dab Lizard (Uromastyx ornata) can be extremely colourful compared with the other species. It is frequently available through the pet trade, although captive-bred individuals are hard to obtain.

Butterfly agamas

The members of this genus are more closely related to the dab lizards (*Uromastyx* species) than to the other agamas, and show certain similarities to them in appearance and behaviour. They can be regarded as slender, fast-moving dab lizards that lack the spiny tails, although their diet is more varied. They are placed in the subfamily Leiolepinae, which consists of just these two genera: *Leiolepis* and *Uromastyx*.

In general, the *Leiolepis* species grow to about 150mm SVL, 450mm TL, although *L. guttata* is somewhat larger. Males and females are of similar size. Their dorsal surface is covered with very small scales, giving them a silky texture, and the scales on the head are only slightly larger. There is no dorsal crest. They are light- to medium-brown, with numerous round white or yellow spots, loosely arranged into rows across their backs. The head is marked with yellow bars and blotches. *L. belliana* has up to nine black bars with patches of bright red between them on its flanks. This characteristic separates this species from other *Leiolepis* species.

Right: The Spotted Butterfly Agama (Leiolepis guttata) is a relatively recent arrival from China. It is the largest species in the genus and its care and breeding are largely unknown, although it is likely to be similar to other members of the genus.

Availability

There are seven species in the genus, of which the Red-sided Butterfly Agama (L. belliana) and Reeve's Butterfly Agama (L. reevesii) have been imported recently. Another species, the Giant Butterfly Agama (L. guttata) has probably been imported from China in the past. This is a larger species than the others, but its requirements appear to be similar, as far as is known. Others may also have been imported from China, but positive identification of some of the more obscure reptiles from that part of the world can be problematic. Parthenogenesis – the ability to reproduce without mating – has been discovered in at least three species, including a form of L. belliana. Non-parthenogenetic species are thought to be monogamous – a vital factor when trying to breed them in captivity.

Leiolepis species are not bred in captivity as far as is known, but imported specimens are often available. These are often heavily parasitised and in poor condition, so they require careful attention if they are to thrive.

Life in the wild

The butterfly agamas are widely distributed in Southeast Asia and southern China, living in open sandy places where they experience the full force of the tropical sun. They live in burrows, which they excavate themselves, and emerge only during the hottest parts of the day. They can flatten their bodies by greatly expanding their ribs, which are not attached at the chest end. This increases the lizard's surface area, allowing it to tilt itself towards the sun and warm up quickly. At the same time, the flank markings – especially in L. belliana – are displayed to their best advantage, hence the name 'butterfly agamas'.

Care in captivity

Butterfly agamas are not difficult to keep once they have overcome the initial period, during which they should be treated for internal parasites and given plenty of security.

Housing Provide a large enclosure at least 1.5m long. Because these agamas are so fast-moving and nervous, all-glass enclosures are not suitable. The enclosure should have at least three solid sides, otherwise the lizards will constantly run into the glass walls and damage themselves. For the same reason, the enclosure should be installed in a secluded position.

Provide a temperature of 25-28°C during the day, with a hot-spot that reaches 40°C. The temperature can be allowed to fall by up to 10°C at night. The lizards prefer a dry, sandy substrate, but also need rocks or logs under which to burrow and retreat. Take care that the rocks cannot collapse on top of them if they are undermined. Spray one area regularly, so that the lizards have somewhere to go if they need a higher humidity – when they are about to shed, for instance. Given these conditions they will calm down in time and become tame.

Feeding The lizards eat insects and vegetation but, like many omnivorous species, prefer to eat insects in captivity. Flowers, especially yellow ones, are more attractive to them than leaves and vegetables.

Breeding Captive-breeding would be an important step forward, as the young would almost certainly adapt to captivity better than adults from the wild. Freshly imported females sometimes lay eggs, the usual clutch consisting of about four eggs. There is no information on incubation or hatching at this time.

Below: The Reeve's Butterfly Agama (Leiolepis reevesii) *has been imported in large numbers in recent years, although there are no records of its breeding in captivity. Acclimatising wild individuals is not easy, but would make a worthwhile project.*

General index

Page numbers in **bold** indicate major entries, including photos; *italics* refer to captions, annotations and panels; plain type indicates other text entries.

Species index

Credits

The publishers would like to thank the following for providing images, credited here by page number and position: (B) Bottom, (T) Top, (C) Centre (BL) Bottom left, etc.

Jason Barnard: 37, 128, 129, 130, 131
Darren Bridgwood: 110, 124, 125, 126, 127(TL,BR)
Rickie Clarke, herpetology specialist (rickie-rep@hotmail.com): 52, 57, 75, 82, 185
Scott Corning: 154-155
Janny Dutemple: *Contents page* 3, 186, 187, 194-195, 195
Lee Grismer: 148-149, 151, 198-199, 201
Guy Haimovitch: 180, 182, 192
Martin Kramer: 16-17(TC)
Ch'ien C. Lee: 147, 152
Chris Mattison: *Title page* (TL,TC,TR), *Contents pages* 4, 5 & 6, 8, 9, 12, 15, 16(BL), 17, 18-19, 20-21, 24, 26(TR,BL), 27, 28-29, 36, 40, 41, 43(T,B), 45, 49(TL,BR), 77, 80, 86, 87, 92, 95(BL,BR), 96(T,C,B), 98, 100, 106(C,B), 108, 109, 111, 112-113(B), 113(T), 114-115, 116-117, 118-119, 121, 123, 132, 133, 135, 136-137, 139, 140-141, 143, 144-145, 157, 158-159, 162-163, 164, 167, 168-169, 171, 181, 188-189, 190-191(T), 191(B), 196-197, 197
Gretchen Mattison: 76(CL)
Erik Paterson: 160, 161(TR,BL)
Tommy Pedersen: 42, 165, 176-177, 179, 193
Aidan Raftery: 88-89(B), 89(TR)
Geoff Rogers © Interpet Publishing: *Title page* (BL,BC,BR), *Contents pages 1 & 2,* 31, 33, 34, 35, 38(T,B), 39, 47(L,TR), 48, 53(BL,TR), 54, 59, 61, 62-74, 76(BC,CR), 78, 79, 81, 83, 84, 93, 102, 103, 104, 105
Ray Wilson: 172-173, 175

Publisher's acknowledgements

The publishers would like to thank the following for their help during the preparation of this book: David Alderton; Swallow Aquatics, East Harling, Norfolk; Wharf Aquatics, Pinxton, Nottinghamshire.

Author's acknowledgements

The author would like to thank the following people who have helped to make this book possible, by supplying information or generously allowing their animals to be photographed, or both. Special thanks to Wayne Swift and Craig Robinson of Wharf Aquatics, who gave unrestricted access to animals and equipment in the shop in Pinxton, Nottinghamshire. John Armitage of the Snake Shop, Sheffield, also helped by loaning animals and equipment and put me in touch with local breeders. Ben Cornick and Jamie Whittaker (J. W. Dragons) allowed me to photograph their superb lizards. Aidan Raftery provided invaluable input on veterinary matters and Scott Corning contributed additional information on breeding Philippine Sailfin Lizards. In addition, it is a pleasure to thank my wife, Gretchen, who accompanied me on several field trips to Africa, Asia and Australia during which I photographed agamid lizards in the wild, and numerous other friends and colleagues who have also provided practical help as well as good company while searching for reptiles in the field. Finally, thanks to all the photographers, listed elsewhere, for submitting images of species and aspects of behaviour that I was not able to obtain.

Publisher's note

The information and recommendations in this book are given without guarantee on the part of the author and publishers, who disclaim any liability with the use of this material.